SERVANT LEADERSHIP NOW

"Stepping-Up Your Leadership Call"

Gardenia T. Bulluck, ACS, BCH.M., M.S. ED.S.

ISBN: 978-1-7330-4730-2 (sc)
ISBN: 978-1-7330473-1-9 (e)

Because of the dynamic nature of the Internet, any web addresses or links contained in this book may have changed
since publication and may no longer be valid. The views expressed in this work are solely those of the author and
do not necessarily reflect the views of the publisher, and the publisher hereby disclaims any responsibility for them.

Any people depicted in stock imagery provided by Getty Images are models,
and such images are being used for illustrative purposes only.
Certain stock imagery © Getty Images.

Scripture quotations taken from The Holy Bible, New International Version® NIV®
Copyright © 1973 1978 1984 2011 by Biblica, Inc. TM. Used by permission. All rights reserved worldwide.

Scripture taken from the New King James Version®. Copyright © 1982 by
Thomas Nelson. Used by permission. All rights reserved.

Lulu Publishing Services rev. date: 10/03/2019

DEDICATION AND ACKNOWLEDGMENTS

I dedicate this book to Our Lord, Jesus the Christ, who is Saviour and Son to The Father. To my biggest earthly cheerleaders, my husband, Sylvester, my godmother Ernestine, my adult children (birthed and God-sent), and of course, my maturing, everyday grandchildren, I am grateful for your supportive ways. Special thanks goes to my brother, Rev. Roderick L. Tillery, Sr., and to a son in the ministry to me, Rev. Keith Butler, who has continued to be encouragers through my ministry endeavors; Special gratitude to Drs. L. Beverly Corridon and Marie Louis who have always been there as prayer warriors; to my faithful early morning prayer partners, for over a decade now, who have continued to be a blessing in my life. Reflectively, I am grateful for those special people who were instrumental in my life and have left their earthly home for a heavenly home: my Soldier Sally, the quiet storm Bea, Mom Mary (the compassionate one) and my strong siblings. I miss you all. I salute Pastor and Lady McRae and the disciples of Abundant Life Ministries of South Florida, who will endure in spite of. Stand on faith! Finally, to Kendra and Courtney - words cannot express how I feel about you. You are rock-solid in Him. You show how a continued stand on His Word to serve others will bring abundance. This is a testament to Servant-Leadership NOW and God's gifting.

I SAY, "THANK YOU."

TABLE OF CONTENTS

INTRODUCTION

Ministry leadership is unique. The primary purpose of this workbook is to support ministry leaders as servant-leaders.

Beginning with the Early Church, church leadership has played a significant role in furthering the kingdom of God. It was through the Church that God revealed the gospel message of Jesus Christ. God's plan includes men and women inspired by the Holy Spirt to share in the message of The Cross. The leadership plan was developed by God. Thus, as servant-leaders, we are called to implement and share in His plan – **His agenda**.

Whether seasoned or new to leadership, it is an exciting time to be **engaged** in the work of **research** and **personal learning** for **ministry**. With this awareness, the activities were designed for you.

The activities are designed to work in **teams or as individuals**. Research shows that leaders learn by doing (experiential learning). The Harvard Business Review (HBR) reported that although organizations spend more than $24 billion annually on leadership development, many leaders who have attended leadership programs **struggle to implement** what they've learned. *It's not because the programs are bad but because leadership is best learned from experience.* **When leaders put knowledge, understanding and experience together, change can be most effective**.

In this text, leaders will engage in *focused work* dedicated to the Word of God by reading and researching scriptures. This will make learning more inspirational and meaningful.

Most of the work activities will highlight leaders in the Biblical text; however, characters from modern time (today) are mentioned as part of reflective study. The intent is to give servant-leaders an exploration of various aspects of leadership at work in behalf of God's Agenda.

For your convenience, in the Appendix section, you will find many of the scriptures for quick study. Several resources are provided in the Attachment section, i.e., Individual, Pastor and Church assessments for summarizing data. A suggestive schedule is also provided for implementing personal and ministry goals.

Blessings!

AUTHOR'S OBJECTIVES

To engage, equip, encourage, evangelize and inspire servant-leaders in the ministry for God's Agenda.

1. Engage
2. Equip
3. Encourage
4. Evangelize &
5. Inspire

The Servant-Leader NOW

For God's Agenda

SECTION I: ASSESSMENTS

ABOUT THE ASSESSMENTS

Knowing who you are and where you are will help you move forward. Assessments in this working text are meant to be supportive and thoughtful tools for spiritual growth. They are not meant to be penalizing. The information gained from the assessments are useful as a **summary** for sharing with the pastor and church body. The numerical rating forms can be used for summarizing the results to confirm specific affirmations and define areas of growth. As a recommendation, there are some types of individual assessments which should **not** be shared. We do this to help distinguish a difference between church growth and spiritual growth, and to promote the usefulness of assessments as tools to gather *truth, integrity, and accountability.* For example, which of the questions are useful for areas of growth for the ministry of the church. Which of the questions are useful for determining spiritual growth as an individual? Although modified, we compared several available assessments and found that the examples presented in this text (from the Northern Plains Region Baptist Conference) could be useful in moving toward ministry objectives.

How often should assessments be taken? At least annually. Pre/post assessments are recommended for comparison and measuring growth.

Should the respondents sign the assessments? Yes. Again, responses are not meant to be penalizing. The pastor should receive a summary without signatures (to reduce the risk of harm) for dialoguing and clarifying issues for resolving.

Guidelines for Assessments

Assessments should be given to persons who work closely with the pastor and who will have leadership roles in the church. Use the assessment summary for further dialoguing and analyzing church needs for spiritual growth. It is recommended that such dialogues take place only after seeking God in prayer.

What is the role of the entire church body? It is important that the entire church body be a part of the process. Inform the body that the pastor and church leaders will be involved in leadership development for the purpose of growing church discipleship; ask the body to pray for the wisdom, grace, and fellowship that will be needed in this process. Praying for the process *should not* be neglected - for the church is accountable for God's kingdom work.

Individual Assessment of the Pastoral Ministry

Page 1 of 4

The purpose of this assessment is to provide the pastor with an overview of ministry. The review is meant to be used constructively to facilitate the pastor's ongoing growth. Keep in mind that the assessment should be prayerfully completed. The results should be summarized and shared with the pastor; however, **Individual Comments (page 2 of this assessment) ARE NOT shared with the pastor.**

1. **How well do you know the pastor? Circle your choice.**
   □ Very Well   □ Well   □ Not Very Well   □ Hardly at all

2. **Is that important to you? Circle your choice.**
   □ Very Important   □ Somewhat important   □ Not at all

3. **What is your level of involvement in the life of the church at present.**
   □ Very involved   □ Somewhat involved   □ Not at all

4. **What limits your involvement?**

5. **Circle one of the following. I have been with this ministry**
   □ More than five years   □ Less than five years

6. **Finally, sign your name to this assessment. Why should you add your name? The answer is "Integrity."**

Individual Assessment of the Pastoral Ministry

Effective leaders are honest and open for growing and reflecting. Leaders who possess integrity gain the trust of team members because he/she does what he/she says he will do and treats others the same way as he/she wants to be treated.

Reminder, this page is NOT shared with the pastor. It will be used for growth development and reflection. This is your reflection.

ADDITIONAL COMMENTS

1. Our pastor does well in the following areas of ministry:

2. The pastor should give more attention to:

3. What do you consider to be the church's responsibilities to the pastor?

4. How have you shown your support to the pastor?

5. If you could say anything you liked to the pastor, what would you say?

Signature_____Date_____

Individual Assessment of the Pastoral Ministry

Page 3 of 4

7. Answer the following questions about the pastoral ministry using the numeric scale.

Numeric Scale:

1 = Disagree Strongly	2 = Disagree	3 = Disagree Somewhat
4 = Agree Somewhat	5 = Agree	6 = Agree Strongly

NOTE: Leave blank if not applicable

PERSONAL LIFE of the pastor						
The pastor gives evidence of:						
1. A deep commitment to Christ and a godly lifestyle.	1	2	3	4	5	6
2. A competent knowledge of the Bible.	1	2	3	4	5	6
3. A love for the work of the church.	1	2	3	4	5	6
4. A concern and compassion for unbelievers.	1	2	3	4	5	6
5. An active prayer life.	1	2	3	4	5	6
HOME LIFE (where applicable)						
6. Takes time with spouse and family.	1	2	3	4	5	6
7. Spouse and family support the ministry.	1	2	3	4	5	6
8. Models a loving home life.	1	2	3	4	5	6
9. Good balance between work/leisure.	1	2	3	4	5	6
10. Allows for recreational time.	1	2	3	4	5	6
AS A LEADER the pastor						
11. Is effective in communicating the vision and goals of the church.	1	2	3	4	5	6
12. Models good time management.	1	2	3	4	5	6
13. Models a spirit of love and a servant attitude.	1	2	3	4	5	6
14. Accepts suggestions well.	1	2	3	4	5	6
15. Supports conference/denominational ministries.	1	2	3	4	5	6
16. Is effective in equipping and empowering the people for ministry.	1	2	3	4	5	6
17. Is aware of and sensitive to peoples' needs.	1	2	3	4	5	6

Individual Assessment of the Pastoral Ministry

Page 4 of 4

Numeric Scale:

1 = Disagree Strongly   2 = Disagree   3 = Disagree Somewhat

4 = Agree Somewhat   5 = Agree   6 = Agree Strongly

NOTE: Leave blank if not applicable

Continued from previous page

AS A COMMUNICATOR *the pastor*						
18. Encourages and challenges me to grow spiritually and mature in my faith.	1	2	3	4	5	6
19. Models the value of prayer.	1	2	3	4	5	6
20. Supports participation in the service.	1	2	3	4	5	6
21. Is biblical and relevant in preaching.	1	2	3	4	5	6
22. Helps me apply biblical truth to my daily life.	1	2	3	4	5	6
23. Is compelling and persuasive in his/her style of delivery.	1	2	3	4	5	6
AS AN ADVISOR/COUNSELLOR *the pastor*						
24. Is easy to talk to.	1	2	3	4	5	6
25. Is a good listener.	1	2	3	4	5	6
26. Is perceptive and understands me.	1	2	3	4	5	6
27. Provides wise counsel and direction.	1	2	3	4	5	6
28. Admits to limits readily.	1	2	3	4	5	6

Pastoral Self-Assessment

Page 1 of 3

To the Pastor: This self-assessment is designed to enhance personal growth. It will help you reflect on your ministry and personal life as well as give direction for goal setting.

1. What has been some of your significant accomplishments this year (ministry and personal)?

2. Are there any aspects of your ministry you would assess as discouraging?

3. What are the strengths of your ministry on which you want to build?

4. What is one key aspect of your ministry you would like to change?

5. How have you worked at developing and mentoring leaders?

6. In what ways have you encouraged and supported other members of your pastoral team?

7. Have you fulfilled the expectations of your job description?

Pastoral Self-Assessment

Page 2 of 3

8. What changes would reflect more accurately your giftedness and ministry?

9. Use the Numeric Scale to answer the questions

Numeric Scale: Pastor Self-Assessment

1 = Strongly Dissatisfied	2 = Dissatisfied	3 = Dissatisfied Somewhat
4 = Satisfied Somewhat	5 = Satisfied	6 = Strongly Satisfied

NOTE: Leave blank if not applicable.

Rate yourself in the following categories:							Comments:
1. Personal devotional life.	1	2	3	4	5	6	
2. Ability to pace myself and take time off.	1	2	3	4	5	6	
3. Relationship with my spouse.	1	2	3	4	5	6	
4. Relationship with my family/ children.	1	2	3	4	5	6	
5. Ability to handle pressure/stress.	1	2	3	4	5	6	
6. Management of personal finances.	1	2	3	4	5	6	
7. Involvement with non-Christians.	1	2	3	4	5	6	
8. Preaching/teaching ministry.	1	2	3	4	5	6	
9. Care/contacting ministry.	1	2	3	4	5	6	
10. Administrative/organizational skills.	1	2	3	4	5	6	

Pastoral Self-Assessment Future Goals

Page 3 of 3

1. In the coming year, I would like to capitalize on the following trend and/ or new opportunities:

2. Three goals that I would like to achieve in the next year:

3. Three goals that I would like to achieve with the church leadership team:

4. What are three goals I would like to see the church body achieve?

   How will they be measured?

Three Goals -Church Body	How Measured	Resources Needed
1.		
2.		
3.		

Additional Comments:

Sign _____ Date _____

Individual Church Ministry Assessment

Page 1 of 2

This assessment will help you reflect on the ministry of the church. As you consider the strengths and weaknesses of the various ministries of the church, it is our hope that you recognize the importance that each member plays in maintaining an effective ministry.

Numeric Scale:

1 = Disagree Strongly   2 = Disagree   3 = Disagree Somewhat

4 = Agree Somewhat   5 = Agree   6 = Agree Strongly

NOTE: Leave blank if not applicable.

WORSHIP						
1. The worship services help us focus our attention on God and His Word.	1	2	3	4	5	6
2. The worship services are uplifting.	1	2	3	4	5	6
3. The style of worship meets the needs and goals of our church.	1	2	3	4	5	6
4. Prayer is viewed as an important part of worship in the church.	1	2	3	4	5	6
PREACHING/TEACHING						
5. Is biblical and relevant to daily life.	1	2	3	4	5	6
6. Provides a clear understanding of God's word.	1	2	3	4	5	6
7. Encourages spiritual growth.	1	2	3	4	5	6
8. Is challenging and motivating.	1	2	3	4	5	6
VISION/LEADERSHIP						
9. The church's vision/mission statement is clearly communicated and known.	1	2	3	4	5	6
10. The pastor & staff have a good working relationship with the church leadership.	1	2	3	4	5	6
11. The leaders are sensitive to the needs of the members and seek their input.	1	2	3	4	5	6
12. Leaders are chosen basis on their spiritual qualifications and ability to lead.	1	2	3	4	5	6
13. I support and regularly pray for our church leaders.	1	2	3	4	5	6
ADMINISTRATION/ORGANIZATION						
14. The organizational structure is effective with clear lines of responsibility/ accountability.	1	2	3	4	5	6
15. Events and services are organized well.	1	2	3	4	5	6
16. Members' needs are cared for through the ministry of the church.	1	2	3	4	5	6

Individual Church Ministry Assessment

Page 2 of 2

DISCIPLESHIP/EQUIPPING						
17. Spiritual growth is taking place through small groups, classes, etc.	1	2	3	4	5	6
18. The church is effective in helping new Christians grow in their faith.	1	2	3	4	5	6
19. Growing in Christlikeness is highly valued and fostered in the church.	1	2	3	4	5	6
20. Training is provided for the various ministries of the church.	1	2	3	4	5	6
21. People are challenged to be involved in ministry and their gifts are affirmed.	1	2	3	4	5	6
22. The purpose of each ministry program is clearly stated.	1	2	3	4	5	6

EVANGELISM/MISSIONS						
23. There is a sense of purpose and direction in reaching our community.	1	2	3	4	5	6
24. Members show a desire to share Christ with their friends.	1	2	3	4	5	6
25. People are coming to Christ through the ministry of the church.	1	2	3	4	5	6
26. The church is committed in prayer and financially to world missions.	1	2	3	4	5	6
27. A good percentage of the church budget is designated for missions.	1	2	3	4	5	6

STEWARDSHIP/FINANCES						
28. The budget appropriately reflects the church's vision and goals for ministry.	1	2	3	4	5	6
29. Biblical stewardship is frequently and effectively taught.	1	2	3	4	5	6
30. I am committed to give proportionally of my income to the church budget.	1	2	3	4	5	6

*Summarizing Form of this information is part of the Attachment Section

Additional Comments:

Signature _____ Date_____

Church Leadership Self-Assessment

Page 1 of 2

The entire leadership team plays a vital role in the quality of ministry. Therefore, it is essential the team be assessed. Please complete the following based on the present: Date_____

Name_____ Position/Role(s) _____

Please read the statement and circle the one that is applicable to you.

I am fulfilled and happy about my position and role on the leadership team.
Most of the time   Sometimes   Hardly ever

I am frustrated about my leadership responsibilities.
Most of the time   Sometimes   Hardly ever

Numeric Scale:

1 = Disagree Strongly   2 = Disagree   3 = Disagree Somewhat
4 = Agree Somewhat   5 = Agree   6 = Agree Strongly

NOTE: Leave blank if not applicable.

1. Our pastoral staff is provided with clear job descriptions.	1	2	3	4	5	6
2. My responsibilities are clearly defined.	1	2	3	4	5	6
3. Ours is a team effort in leadership.	1	2	3	4	5	6
4. Our pastoral staff is adequately supported financially.	1	2	3	4	5	6
5. I am modeling godliness in lifestyle, financial stewardship, and faithfulness in service.	1	2	3	4	5	6

Church Leadership Self-Assessment

1. The strengths I bring to my role as a leader of this church are:

2. The strengths in the life of this ministry as a congregation are:

3. What areas of congregational life need change and growth?

4. I would like to see our congregation grow in the next one to three years in the following ways:

5. The three areas where the church needs to put the greatest emphasis are:

Signature _____ Date _____

Why should I add my name? Integrity

Effective leaders are honest and open for growing and reflecting. Leaders who possess integrity gain the trust of team members because he/she does what he/she says he will do and treats others the same way as he/she wants to be treated.

SECTION II: CHARACTER TRAITS ACTIVITIES

In the Character/Traits section, you will read an old tale; review leadership traits; review wise behaviors based on the Book of Proverbs; reflect upon statements from world leaders; engage in activities related to the content and finally, state your takeaways.

CONTENT LESSONS AND ACTIVITIES

Don't Blame It on Adam
❖ Activity #1 – Hiding Out
❖ Activity #2 – The Blame Game

Effective Researched Leadership Traits
❖ Activity #3 – Your Leadership Values

Types of Common Leadership Styles
❖ Activity #4 – The Servant Leadership Style

Proverbial Wisdom & Wise Behaviors
❖ Activity #5 – The Call for Prudence
❖ Activity #6 – The Call for Understanding
❖ Character Traits in Proverbs Chart 2
❖ Activity #7 – Proverbial Traits in Action

Reflective Views from World Leaders
❖ Activity #8 – Leadership Thoughts and Counsel

Personal Takeaways

Don't Blame It On Adam

Author Unknown

A story about a poor woodcutter believes he would be living a life of ease if Adam had not been banished from the Garden of Eden.

There once was a poor woodcutter named Iyapo who lived on the edge of a village in a small hut. Every morning he rose early and went into the forest to chop wood. He would bundle it up and carry it to town to sell.

He was not able to eat breakfast until after he sold some wood; then he would have enough money to buy something to eat. As he walked through the streets, he yelled, "Wood, Wood, who will buy some of this wood?" "Wood, Wood, it's all the fault of Adam that we have good wood for sale."

One day as he was selling his wood, the king heard Iyapo's strange words. "Who is this person that yells out such a thing?" "Why does he say that it is the fault of Adam? As king, if anyone has done him, then I should know about it."

The king's adviser asks the other officers but none of them knew why Iyapo would say such a thing. So the officers took Iyapo to the king for further inquiry. The poor woodcutter feared for his situation. He fell on the floor before the king out of both fear and respect.

"Tell me, woodcutter, what is your name?" inquired the king.

"I am Iyapo, oh King."

"Your name, Iyapo means 'many troubles,' but why are you blaming Adam?"

"I heard long ago how Adam disobeyed God and ate the forbidden fruit. If he had not done such a thing, we would all now be living in the Garden of Eden and I would never go hungry. That is why I blame Adam for my situation."

"I see. Your work is hard, yet you go hungry. It really does not seem fair. Because of Adam's mistake you are in such a state. As your king, I will be glad to help you."

The king called his adviser. "Have Iyapo washed and dressed in fine clothes. Then bring him to the palace and let him stay in one of the rooms there. He will have a new life. No more rags and wood will he have to sell for food."

"Iyapo, from now on I will be a brother to you. We will share everything. You can do anything you like except one thing – you may not open the door at the end of the hall. That is the one thing you may never do. Do you understand?"

"Oh, my king, thank you. That is clear. But why should I open such a door when I have everything I need? I have clothes, food, shelter, a wonderful friend in you. What more could I want?"

And so, the woodcutter began a life of comfort. He no longer had to work hard for his food or want for the comforts of life. He even forgot about the green door until one day he passed by it.

Awe. This was the green door he was never to open. He wondered why. Why would the king's brother not be allowed to open the door? What was in the room behind the door? He wondered but he went on.

In the next days, Iyapo grew more curious about the door. Several times during the day, he found himself standing outside the door and each time he was getting more and more curious. Sometimes, he even moved his hand toward the door handle but he managed to stop himself from opening the door.

One day, the king said, "Brother, I have been called away to another town, and I will be gone for a while but I will be back late today. I am entrusting you to keep the palace while I am away. Make sure all is well."

After the king letf, the woodcutter started thinking how good it would be to see what was behind the door. "I am responsible for the room behind the green door as well. I must as the king's brother make sure all is well. I must go and find out what is hidden there."

After checking that no one was looking, Iyapo put his ear against the door. He could not hear a thing.

"I must know what is in the room. I will just open the door a little, a crack, and peek inside. Then I will close it again. The king will never know."

And so Iyapo gently and slightly opened the door. The room was dark. After a while, he could see the old rags he used to wear and the wood he used to sell. All of a sudden, a mouse ran out the door.

"Oh, no!" cried Iyapo. "The king was hiding a mouse in the room and now it has escaped. I must catch it and return it to the room. As he ran after the mouse, his shoes fell off. He tripped over his long, beautiful robe and had to take it off. Still, he could not catch the mouse. Hot and out of breath, he found it harder and harder to catch such a creature. Suddenly, there appeared the king. He had returned from his journey.

"What are you doing, Iyapo?" "Why are you out of breath?" "Why are you without your clothes?"

Poor Iyapo threw himself before the king's feet and begin to cry out, "I'm sorry." "I did not mean to let your mouse go."

"What mouse?" asked the king. "I have no mouse."

"The mouse in the room. When I opened the green door, the mouse…"

"You opened the green door?"

"I did not mean to. I was wrong, but my feet kept taking me there and there and there and there. I was so curious and…"

"Iyapo, I am very sorry for you. I am disappointed in you. Opening the green door was the one thing I told you not to do."

"I know, kind sire, but I am the brother of the king and …"

"And now you want to be the king himself," shouted the king. "You are worse than Adam. You should have learned from his mistake."

"I am sorry, my lord. It will not happen again, I promise. What do you wish me to do?"

The king's anger had disappeared. Now he had tears in his eyes. "Go back to the room. You must now take your rags and sticks of woods. You must return to the market and sell your wood to eat and have shelter.

"Yes, sire," was all the woodcutter could say.

"And remember this – others cannot make you happy. It is up to you and your fate. Go and work hard and know that your poverty is not the fault of Adam or anyone else."

And so Iyapo returned to the market. Once again he shouted, "Wood for sale. Who wants to buy good wood?" But he never mentioned Adam again.

Iyapo – Observable and Unobservable Traits

Several traits of Iyapo are quite observable and others were not observable based on his statements and actions. Examples of visible and invisible traits include:

- ❏ **Finger-pointing** (opposite of responsible) - "I heard long ago how Adam disobeyed God and ate the forbidden fruit. If he had not done such a thing, we would all now be living in the Garden of Eden and I would never go hungry. That is why I blame Adam for my situation."

- ❏ **Dishonesty** (opposite of integrity) - "I am responsible for the room behind the green door as well. I must as the king's brother make sure all is well. I must go and find out what is hidden there."

  It is true that Iyapo was entrusted to keep the palace while the king was away, however, his curiosity overruled his integrity. In the next days, Iyapo grew more curious about the door. Several times during the day, he found himself standing outside the door and each time he was getting more and more curious.

- ❏ **Disrespectful** (opposite of respectful) – "I did not mean to. I was wrong, but my feet kept taking me there and there and there and there. I was so curious and…"

  "Iyapo, I am very sorry for you. I am disappointed in you. Opening the green door was the one thing I told you not to do."

The following activities "Hiding Out" and "The Blame Game" will give you an opportunity to reflect upon your personal traits and responses.

Activity #1 Hiding Out

Not all the time are we aware of our responses until certain situations occur (like Iyapo). Sometimes, it is not until we are faced with such circumstances that we discover or rediscover hidden traits and are surprised by our responses. So to say, "If I was you, I would do it this way or that way," may not be a wise statement. It may be that we would do just that very thing.

God allows us to develop by permitting certain circumstances to occur which will reveal truths that otherwise we would not know (Jeremiah 29:11). Has it ever happened that you believed you had overcome a habit only to discover that you have not? We can thank God for His protection in these instances and know that God wants us to recognize our fears, strengths, and challenges. He desires that we confront our personal issues and get well - HEAL. 1 Corinthians 10:13 NKJV reads, "No temptation has overtaken you except such as is common to man; but God is faithful, who will not allow you to be tempted beyond what you are able, but with the temptation will also make the way of escape, that you may be able to bear it."

The Bible narrates the stories of imperfect leaders who were called and chose to "hide out." Examples of those who sought to hide out and not face their challenges include Adam, David, Elijah, and Jonah. When God allows us as Prodigal Sons and Daughters to recover from our mistakes, gives us another opportunity because of His grace and mercy, we owe Him praise and service.

REFLECTIVE QUESTIONS

(1) Look up the following Scriptures related to "hiding" and write out the Scriptures:

Genesis 3:8

_____

_____

Jeremiah 16:17

_____

_____

Jeremiah 23:24

_____

_____

Hebrews 4:13

_____

_____

(2) Under what circumstances have you felt that "hiding out" was the answer to your problem?

_____

_____

(3) Was this a positive thing to do for your situation? Why or Why Not?

_____

_____

(4) What did you learn from the experience?

_____

_____

Activity #2 The Blame Game

Playing the "blame game" can cause unexpected consequences. In the story, 'Don't Blame It on Adam,' Iyapo blamed his situation on Adam. His excuse kept him in poverty. It affected his actions and responses in life.

God wants his leaders to be effective. He knows that we sometimes allow people and things to get in the way of personal progress. Not all circumstances are necessarily of our own personal doing; for instance, where one is born, where one lives or choice of an ethnic background. On the other hand, there are situations that can be directly attributable to us, especially when it hinders us from moving forward. An example could be the choice of friends we make or refusal to seek available help to kick an unhealthy habit.

The blame game, as we saw in the story, can hold you back, which is a good reason to institute *change*.

In leadership AND in life, change is necessary for growth. You cannot stay in "first grade" forever. PROMOTION IS NECESSARY FOR GRADUATION.

It is important to reflect upon milestones to make required changes, i.e., where have I been, where do I need to go, and how do I get there. We cannot allow blame to stop our connections in moving forward because God is necessary and available to help. So let's reflect to ensure blame is not a stumbling block for improving your calling and service in leadership.

REFLECTIVE QUESTIONS

(1) What or who is/was the blame for your not accepting a position or challenge? You do not have to share your answers with others, but "to thine own self be truthful."

_____

_____

_____

_____

(2) How has this impacted your life? Your ministry? Your leadership?

Life: _____

Ministry _____

Leadership: _____

(3) **How can or did you effectively change the situation?**

_____

_____

(4) **On a scale from 1 to 5, and 5 is the highest, how badly is your desire to seek the Holy Spirit for guidance to change a situation?**

_____

_____

_____

_____

(5) **Does my situation require a change in me?**

    a. Yes   b. No

When?

    a. Now   b. Wait

(6) **Empower Your Learning**

Listen to what the Holy Spirit is saying (and not what you want to hear). Open your heart to God NOW. Keep a "journal" of what you hear as you work through the situation.

A prayer life is essential to the change. Simply thank Him and ask for revelation to resolve your issue and make the necessary change(s).

What am I willing to give up in order to develop my prayer life during prayer time with the Father? i.e., phone time, conversations during that hour, etc.

As I Go Through Change

Dear God,

I love you, Lord, my strength. The Lord is my rock, my fortress and my deliverer; my God is my rock, in whom I take refuge, my shield and the horn of my salvation, my stronghold. Psalm 18:1-2NIV

Special Scriptures I was led to read;

---

(7) Reflection: What did you learn by listening to the Holy Spirit?
Expect God to reveal things you may not like. Use the space provided. Write to thank God for the Holy Spirit revealing, guiding, and teaching you in change; thank God for walking with you as a servant of His.

(a) Reflection: Is the situation related to family, ministry, relationship(s) or work?

(b) Is the situation impacting other area(s) of your life?

(c) Does the situation require professional help?

(d) What did I refine or change so that I could develop prayer time with the Father?

Effective Researched Leadership Traits Chart 1

According to several research studies, effective leaders have in common certain traits or characteristics and those traits encourage others to follow leaders. Some people naturally possess these traits, i.e., compassion and integrity; while others need formal training in the acquisition of specific traits. Whether naturally or formally acquired, the success of organizations depends upon specific characteristics. Listed below are ten qualities professionals have endorsed to inspire trust, respect and stimulate production within a workplace or organization.

Communication

Effective leaders communicate clearly. Understanding the consequences of verbal and written communication skills allow leaders to present and perceive expected outcomes to individual/team actions. Successful leaders focus on developing communication skills for listening to others rather than "talking to be heard."

Organization

Effective leaders possess exceptional organizational skills. Organizational skills help leaders plan objectives and strategies. This will allow team members to perform at the optimal level of leadership. Organized leaders put systems in place that maintain order and guide members toward meeting goals and objectives.

Confidence

Effective leaders are confident in their abilities and aim to develop and place confidence in the abilities of the team. Confident leaders are secure in their decisions that affect the team. Leaders reassure the team confidence in their ability to carry out the mission.

Respectful

Leaders are respectful of his/her team members. Leaders empower members by encouraging them to offer ideas about decisions that affect the mission; members will appreciate that the leader respects their input and opinions.

Fair

Leaders treat team members with fairness – honorably. Rewards and recognition are equally displayed. Disciplinary action is administered fairly but with consideration of the team member's ability to handle treatment.

Integrity

Effective leaders are honest and open with team members. Leaders who possess integrity gain the trust of team members because he/she does what he/she says he will do and treats others the same way as he/she wants to be treated.

Influential

Influential leaders help inspire the commitment of team members to meet goals and objectives. Influential leaders also help manage change within the organization. Leaders help by gaining the confidence of members through effective decision making and communication.

Delegation

Effective leaders know how to share leadership through delegation. Delegating certain tasks to trustworthy team members allows the leader to focus on improving functions and production.

Facilitator

Effective leaders are powerful facilitators. As a facilitator, team leaders help members understand their goals. They also help organize an action plan to ensure team members meet their goals and objectives more efficiently.

Negotiation

Leaders utilize negotiation skills to achieve results and reach an understanding in the event of a conflict. Leaders who negotiate effectively streamline the decision-making process, as well as solve problems for the best interest of everyone involved.

In any organization, these ten traits may be represented as interchangeable terms, i.e., positive attitude, competence, empowerment, passion, curiosity, vision, values, etc. But the meaning does not change nor does the purpose of the traits/characteristics.

When we speak of an organization, we immediately envision an organized body of people with a particular purpose, i.e., business. However, when we speak of a church, we envision a body of people organized for a godly purpose.

There are perceived expectations and outcomes in both environments. The world's system has categorized a list of the most common leadership styles based on the desired characteristics or functions. There exists in both (secular and church system) a hierarchy to accomplish objectives, missions, expectations or goals. Moreover, much of the secular systems stem from biblical principles, i.e., moral and ethical values. Factually, a level of hierarchy and character traits were operating at the beginning of Creation i.e., *wisdom, negotiation, communication, passion, attitude, empowerment, integrity, etc.* Examples of these values are throughout the Bible for God is a Spirit. Wisdom existed from the beginning through Him. In Him, these traits (fair, delegation, organization, facilitation, etc.) are identifiable and are not erased.

In the beginning was God! The Organizer, Communicator, and all the traits assisted through Him – Wisdom.

[1] In the beginning God created the heavens and the earth. [2] Now the earth was formless and empty, darkness was over the surface of the deep, and the Spirit of God was hovering over the waters.

[3] And God said, "Let there be light," and there was light. [4] God saw that the light was good, and he separated the light from the darkness. [5] God called the light "day," and the darkness he called "night." And there was evening, and there was morning—the first day.

[6] And God said, "Let there be a vault between the waters to separate water from water." [7] So God made the vault and separated the water under the vault from the water above it. And it was so. [8] God called the vault "sky." And there was evening, and there was morning—the second day.

[9] And God said, "Let the water under the sky be gathered to one place, and let dry ground appear." And it was so. [10] God called the dry ground "land," and the gathered waters he called "seas." And God saw that it was good.

[11] Then God said, "Let the land produce vegetation: seed-bearing plants and trees on the land that bear fruit with seed in it, according to their various kinds." And it was so. [12] The land produced vegetation: plants bearing seed according to their kinds and trees bearing fruit with seed in it according to their kinds. And God saw that it was good. [13] And there was evening, and there was morning—the third day.

¹⁴ And God said, "Let there be lights in the vault of the sky to separate the day from the night, and let them serve as signs to mark sacred times, and days and years, ¹⁵ and let them be lights in the vault of the sky to give light on the earth." And it was so. ¹⁶ God made two great lights—the greater light to govern the day and the lesser light to govern the night. He also made the stars. ¹⁷ God set them in the vault of the sky to give light on the earth, ¹⁸ to govern the day and the night, and to separate light from darkness. And God saw that it was good. ¹⁹ And there was evening, and there was morning—the fourth day.

²⁰ And God said, "Let the water teem with living creatures, and let birds fly above the earth across the vault of the sky." ²¹ So God created the great creatures of the sea and every living thing with which the water teems and that moves about in it, according to their kinds, and every winged bird according to its kind. And God saw that it was good. ²² God blessed them and said, "Be fruitful and increase in number and fill the water in the seas, and let the birds increase on the earth." ²³ And there was evening, and there was morning—the fifth day.

²⁴ And God said, "Let the land produce living creatures according to their kinds: the livestock, the creatures that move along the ground, and the wild animals, each according to its kind." And it was so. ²⁵ God made the wild animals according to their kinds, the livestock according to their kinds, and all the creatures that move along the ground according to their kinds. And God saw that it was good.

²⁶ Then God said, "Let us make mankind in our image, in our likeness, so that they may rule over the fish in the sea and the birds in the sky, over the livestock and all the wild animals,[a] and over all the creatures that move along the ground."

²⁷ So God created mankind in his own image, in the image of God he created them; male and female he created them.

²⁸ God blessed them and said to them, "Be fruitful and increase in number; fill the earth and subdue it. Rule over the fish in the sea and the birds in the sky and over every living creature that moves on the ground."

²⁹ Then God said, "I give you every seed-bearing plant on the face of the whole earth and every tree that has fruit with seed in it. They will be yours for food. ³⁰ And to all the beasts of the earth and all the birds in the sky and all the creatures that move along the ground—everything that has the breath of life in it—I give every green plant for food." And it was so.

³¹ God saw all that he had made, and it was very good. And there was evening, and there was morning—the sixth day.

Genesis 1: 1-31 NIV

Activity #3 Your Leadership Values

(1) Do we conform and acknowledge these traits in Chart 1 were in existence from the beginning of Creation? Now, based on the list of effective leadership traits in Chart #1, rank the traits in the order you value most in leaders.

10_____   5 _____

9 _____   4 _____

8 _____   3 _____

7 _____   2 _____

6 _____   1 _____

(2) Which trait do you believe is your highest strength?_____

(3) Is that trait naturally or formally acquired? _____

(4) Is the trait you value the most the same trait that is your highest strength? _____

(5) What trait(s) challenge you? _____

(6) Can this trait(s) be formally acquired?_____

(7) How can you acquire this trait(s)?_____

(8) Give at least one example of when you doubted your strength as a leader?

_____

_____

_____

_____

(9) How did you overcome the challenge? If not, why?

_____

_____

(10) What resources were of value to you in this situation?

_____

_____

(11) What resources were needed but you did not have access to these resources?

(12) God is our Source. At what point did you reach out to the Source?

_____

_____

(13) Is there an identifiable trait in you that hindered or helped you in your crisis?

_____

_____

(14) Is this trait one that you feel empowered to magnify in your leadership?

_____

_____

(15) How?

_____

_____

(16) What Scripture can you offer in support of this trait?

_____

_____

Types of Common Leadership Styles

In leadership, we categorize methods that leaders use in order to motivate, implement, and monitor the effectiveness of those they lead. This gives workers an identifiable method of understanding what type of leadership are most effective that drives or inspire them. It helps in treatment, decision-making, communication, and establishing goals. The following is a list of common leadership styles identified by Human Resource Managers, companies or organizations.

Autocratic – This style of leadership give managers total authority to make decisions alone without any input of others. Decisions are not challenge but followed.

Bureaucratic – Leadership is based on hierarchy of authority; fixed rules and duties; highly regulated; does not require must creativity or innovation from its workers. Rules govern the environment, employees and managers' behaviors and possesses.

Laissez-Faire – Highly skilled and trained employees are required to work with little supervisor; limited interference by supervisors or managers; can cause a laxed atmosphere that hinders success.

Participative – Another name for this style of leadership is democratic. Input from team members is expected; decision making is team-focused; leadership is motivating; delegation and opinions are accepting; works well when a short-term decision must be made quickly; employees feel valued.

Systematic – Leadership is the combination of management and employee working for a common goal; complicated and challenging because of its model approach for inclusiveness and valuing input from all; push for creativity, production, and fairness to resolve complex issues; intrinsic and outward rewards; critical thinking and reflective thinking.

Transactional – Managers engage in specific tasks; evaluation takes place at the managerial level; performance-based; provide rewards and punishments based on performance; result-oriented; predetermined organization and employee goals; employees are compensated for accomplishments.

Transformational – Leadership is driven by high levels of communication via managers; leadership is motivating and contributing; requires efficient and effective communication; consists of long-term, specific goals; goal-oriented staff to increase production; smaller tasks are delegated to accomplish goals.

Activity #4 The Servant Leadership Style

There is a push in some corporate organizations to view this type of leadership as a positive direction for the reinvention of the executive model. An example is the Y-Scout company. Their ideas is identifying desired character traits of executives will help make a business successful. These traits are *empathy, listening, awareness, healing, conceptualization, persuasive, stewardship, foresight, community building, and committed growth to other*s. The servant leadership model does not work for all business organizations because MISSION is the focus.

Non-profits are usually the successful benefactors of the Servant Leadership model; it is the embedded culture of these organizations that makes the difference. Like many organizations, those who implement the Servant-Leadership style benefit from various traits of other styles; but success of the organization is shaped by the MISSION.

As to the Church, the *servant's goal is to give service that will please God by addressing the needy*; **service that will address NEED.** Servant leaders are expected to operate with a very high attitude of integrity and generosity. Decision-making is more group focused than independent. Leadership must be aimed by a commitment to help its members direct their energy toward the vision and purpose of the ministry.

REFLECTIVE QUESTIONS

(1) Take a "second look" at the list of Common Leadership styles in Chart 1. What leadership style is most recognizable to you?

_____

_____

(2) What has been the most effective leadership style for you and 'Why?'

_____

_____

_____

_____

(3) What combination of common leadership styles do you prefer?

_____

_____

_____

_____

(4) Is the leadership style(s) you prefer connected to the traits you most value?

_____

_____

_____

_____

(5) What problem(s) can you envision that may arise or have risen when a Servant Leader tries to approach a spiritual matter using a secular (worldly) approach?

_____

_____

_____

_____

Wisdom Is More than Knowledge

"Instruct the wise and they will become wiser still; teach the righteous and they will add to their learning," (Proverbs 9:9 NIV).

I remember as a child, watching my father (who was not a mechanic by trade) work on different types of automobiles - his own, neighbors and other people who would drive from other areas for his expertise. He did NOT have an automotive manual or book, rather he had to rely upon his own skill – a systematic process until he resolved the issue. That was wisdom!

Most people would define wisdom as intelligence. If asked what represents wisdom, answers will vary. Millions view the best examples of man's wisdom as The Great Pyramids of Giza, Saint Peter's Basilica, The Great Wall of China or the Colosseum of Rome. There are those who would probably rank space travel and medical breakthroughs as examples of wisdom.

The Bible tells us that true wisdom had its beginning with God. He brought order through systematized processes beyond human intellect. Out of chaos, He alone created an order which governs the world; we view it through the various sciences referring to the study of, for example, human, economics, geography, biological, and technology. God in His infinite wisdom created wonders among, around and for His purpose.

God summons his servants to be wise and disciplined. In fact, God's faithful servants are encouraged to ask for this type of wisdom (James 1:5). Solomon asked for such wisdom to govern the people of Israel with justice, judgment, and equity; (I Kings 3 and Proverbs 1). If we are to be true representatives of God, we will NOT shun His wisdom; we will seek it.

From the Old Testament, we have the wisdom of Job, Psalm, Ecclesiastes, Song of Solomon and The Book of Proverbs (known as The Wisdom Books). Before the days of Israel's kings, God affirmed Judges who spoke His wisdom. Hebrew 1 tells us that God used Prophets (i.e., Isaiah, Jeremiah) to speak His wisdom. 'God, who at various times and in various ways spoke in time past to the fathers by the prophets," Hebrews 1:1 NKJV. God sent His son to speak wisdom: "has in these last days spoken to us by *His* Son, whom He has appointed heir of all things, through whom also He made the worlds."

The standard of living talked about in these Books is meant to teach moral character and to teach us how to live. Continuingly, God provides mankind with the gift of insight to bring order out of chaos for gaining wisdom and instruction; for understanding words of insight, Proverbs 1:2. Much is to be learned and gained through proverbs, parables and human experiences to enhance wisdom.

The Wisdom Books are not short either on instructions about listening. The art of listening is a connection to obedience to God. "*Listen*, my son, to your father's instruction, and do not forsake your mother's teaching," Proverbs 1:8. This wisdom is amplified from the willingness to *hear* from those who speak wisdom (Proverbs 13). An honest witness tells the truth, but a false witness tells lies (Proverbs 12:17). Therefore, following the lies of false witnesses leads to disobedience for many do choose and practice evil to bring harm. They make this choice over good.

False witnesses come in various means at various times for various reasons. "The lips of the wise spread knowledge, but the hearts of fools are not upright," Proverbs 15:7. 'Good people obtain favor from the lord, but he condemns those who devise wicked schemes,' (Proverbs 12:2 NIV). Those on God's agenda are to be discerners as to not cause harm and ruin but bring order to your environment, i.e., family, workplace, community and ministry. How does one obtain Wisdom that is more than knowledge…

Ask God for wisdom that brings understanding - for Wisdom is more than knowledge.

Proverbial Wisdom of Wise Behaviors

From The Book of Proverbs

God is Wisdom. As the book of Genesis describes - In His wisdom there are principles of creativity, negotiation, communication, passion, attitude, empowerment, integrity, decision-making, fairness/equity, and judgment/justice. The Wisdom Book of Proverbs is filled with principles. A true proverb will move an individual toward the acquisition of godly values. Examples of proverbial wisdom begin with Proverbs 1.

Proverbs 1:1-7 NKJV

1 The proverbs of Solomon the son of David, king of Israel:

2 To know wisdom and instruction, To perceive the words of understanding,

3 To receive the instruction of wisdom, justice, judgment, and equity;

4 To give prudence to the simple,

To the young man knowledge and discretion—

5 A wise *man* will hear and increase learning,

And a man of understanding will attain wise counsel,

6 To understand a proverb and an enigma,

The words of the wise and their riddles.

7 The fear of the LORD *is* the beginning of knowledge,

But fools despise wisdom and instruction.

On a personal note, I recall a teaching from my fraternal grandmother, *"Don't let your ear be a trash can for others."* **Over time, I did come to a better understanding of this saying. It took going through obstacles and pain, but I am appreciative of the lessons learned.**

Proverbs 1:20-30 NKJV – When You Reject Wisdom

20 Wisdom calls aloud outside;

She raises her voice in the open squares.

21 She cries out in the chief concourses,

At the openings of the gates in the city

She speaks her words:

22 "How long, you simple ones, will you love simplicity?

For scorners delight in their scorning, And fools hate knowledge.

23 Turn at my rebuke;

Surely I will pour out my spirit on you; I will make my words known to you.

24 Because I have called and you refused, I have stretched out my hand and no one regarded,

25 Because you disdained all my counsel, And would have none of my rebuke,

26 I also will laugh at your calamity; I will mock when your terror comes,

27 When your terror comes like a storm, And your destruction comes like a whirlwind, When distress and anguish come upon you.

28 "Then they will call on me, but I will not answer; They will seek me diligently, but they will not find me.

29 Because they hated knowledge And did not choose the fear of the Lord,

30 They would have none of my counsel *And* despised my every rebuke.

REFLECTION

Good or bad, how has the lack of wisdom affected your decisions, direction, or leadership?

_____

_____

Wisdom Adorns Righteousness

Proverbs 13:1-3 NKJV

[1] A wise son heeds his father's instruction, But a scoffer does not listen to rebuke.

[2] A man shall eat well by the fruit of his mouth, But the soul of the unfaithful feeds on violence.

[3] He who guards his mouth preserves his life, But he who opens wide his lips shall have destruction.

**"The lips of the wise spread knowledge, but
the hearts of fools are not upright,"
Proverbs 15:7 NKJV.**

REFLECTION

In what ways have you witnessed Proverbs 15:7? What was the situation, cause and effect?

Situation:

Cause:

Effect:

What was the resolution and/or lesson learned?

Solution:

Activity #5 Proverbs and The Call for Prudence

To give prudence to the simple,
To the young man knowledge and discretion, Proverbs 1:4 NKJV

Servant leadership calls for prudence. Prudence is defined as care, caution and good judgment. The leader must look ahead (discern) and listen to God for administering prudence.

As a servant leader, under what circumstances do you believe you will need to exercise prudence based on the definition?

Care: Where can you administer care?

_____

_____

_____

Caution: Under what circumstances can you administer caution?

_____

_____

_____

Good judgment: How can you administer good judgment?

_____

_____

_____

Proverbs 2:1-9 NKJV

[1]My son, if you receive my words, And treasure my commands within you,
[2] So that you incline your ear to wisdom, *And* apply your heart to understanding;
[3]Yes, if you cry out for discernment, *And* lift up your voice for understanding,

[4] If you seek her as silver, And search for her as *for* hidden treasures;
[5] Then you will understand the fear of the Lord, And find the knowledge of God

[6] For the Lord gives wisdom; From His mouth *come* knowledge and understanding;
[7] He stores up sound wisdom for the upright; *He is* a shield to those who walk uprightly;

[8] He guards the paths of justice, And preserves the way of His saints.
[9] Then you will understand righteousness and justice, Equity *and* every good path.

REFLECTION

Previously, we stated that real success comes from listening to the instructions of God. The above Proverbs pronounces that "if" one does certain things "then" there are fruits to be given. Reflect upon how do you at this time in your life (NOW) apply your heart for listening to God?

_____

_____

Read 1 Kings 3 and then reflect upon your words from the above verses 8-9. What are your thoughts about God?

_____

_____

Activity #6 Proverbs and The Call for Understanding

REFLECTIVE QUESTIONS

(1) "So that you incline your ear to wisdom, *And* apply your heart to understanding," Proverbs 2:2 NKJV.

The word "And" denotes that there is something to be gained from wisdom. This is pause for understanding.

If you incline your ear to wisdom, without understanding, what do you think will be the result of your leadership? Wisdom without understanding will:

_____

_____

(2) Read the following from Proverbs 4:5-9

5 Get wisdom! Get understanding! Do not forget, nor turn away from the words of my mouth.
6 Do not forsake her, and she will preserve you; Love her, and she will keep you.
7 Wisdom *is* the principal thing; *Therefore* get wisdom. And in all your getting, get understanding.
8 Exalt her, and she will promote you; She will bring you honor, when you embrace her.
9 She will place on your head an ornament of grace; A crown of glory she will deliver to you.

What is the principal thing? _____

Why understanding? _____

(3) On a scale of 1-10, and 10 being the highest, how important was *understanding* to you before reading these verses? After reading these verses? Was there a change?

_____

_____

(4) Give an example when lack of understanding hindered your progress or success.

_____

_____

(5) What is/was the reason for your lack of understanding?

_____

_____

(6) How did it affect you and other(s)?

_____

_____

(7) When learning from a mistake, based on scriptural foundations, how can you move toward wisdom and understanding?

_____

_____

(8) You previously reflected about Solomon praying for wisdom (1 Kings 3:1-15). Examine what he said in verse 9, "_Therefore give to Your servant an understanding heart to judge Your people, that I may discern between good and evil. For who is able to judge this great people of Yours?_"

He seems to know that his age was problematic in his decision-making. Why might this be a problem in leadership?

_____

_____

_____

Character Traits In Proverbs Chart 2

TRAITS TO BE PROMOTED		TRAITS TO BE AVOIDED	
Avoidance of strife	20:3	Anger	29:22
Compassion for animals	12:10	Antisocial behavior	18:1
Contentment	13:5; 14:30; 15:27	Beauty without discretion	11:22
Diligence	6:6; 12:24,27; 13:4	Dishonesty	24:28
Faithful love	20:6	Greed	28:25
Faithfulness	3:5-6; 5:15-17; 25:13; 28:20	Hatred	29:27
Generosity	21:26; 22:9	Hot temper	19:19; 29:22
Honesty	16:11; 24:26	Immorality	6:20-25
Humility	11:2; 16:19; 25:6-7; 29:23	Inappropriate desire	27:7
Integrity	11:3; 25:26; 28:18	Injustice	22:16
Kindness to others	11:16-17	Jealousy	27:4
Kindness to enemies	25:21-22	Lack of mercy	21:13
Leadership	30:19-31	Laziness	6:6-11; 18:9; 19:15; 20:4; 24:30-34; 26:13-15
Loyalty	19:22	Maliciousness	6:27
Nobility	12:4; 31:10,29	Meddling	26:17; 30:10
Patience	15:18; 16:32	Pride	15:5; 16:18; 21:4,24; 29:23; 30:13

Traits in Proverbs Continued

Peacefulness	16:7	Quarrelsomeness	26:21
Praiseworthiness	27:21	Self-conceit	26:12,16
Righteousness	4:26-27; 11:5-6,30; 12:28; 13:6; 29:2	Self-deceit	28:11
Self-control	17:27; 25:28; 29:11	Self-glory	25:27
Strength and honor	20:29	Self-righteousness	30:12
Strength in adversity	24:10	Social disruption	19:10
Teachable	15:31	Stubbornness	29:1
Truthfulness	12:19,22; 23:23	Unfaithfulness	25:19
		Un-neighborliness	3:27-30
		Vengeance	24:28-29
		Wickedness	21:10
		Wicked scheming	16:30

Source: Adapted from Expositor's Bible Commentary – Abridged Edition: The Old Testament by Kenneth L. Barker; John R. Kohlenberger III. Copyright 1994 by the Zondervan Corporation. Used by permission of Zondervan.

Activity #7 Proverbial Traits In Action

(1) From Chart 2, *Character Traits Found in Proverbs,* a number of traits are listed. What trait(s) have you seem exited among leaders that you most admire in difficult situations?

_____

(2) Choose a trait(s) you want to promote. Choose a trait(s) you want to avoid.
Promote:_____
Avoid:_____

(3) Based on your answer in question #2, where can you apply this trait for experiential learning to improve your leadership i.e., home, family, church? _____

(4) Solomon asked God for an understanding heart with wisdom. What is your inquiry?. It is not too late to ask NOW!

"Keep me safe, my God, for in you I take refuge. I say to the Lord, "You are my Lord; apart from you I have no good thing," Psalm 16:1-2 NIV.

For improvement in the area(s) of my life, I pray…. In the name of Jesus.

Activity #8 – Witnessing Leadership and Wisdom

My maternal grandmother was considered in the community as a wise, nurturing woman of God. In fact, although my fraternal grandmother was older than my maternal grandmother, my fraternal grandmother always addressed her as "Ms." In their time, preceding one's name with the title of "Ms." was a symbol of honor.

I recall when the "men on the block" called for a "fast" when my maternal grandmother passed on to meet Our Maker. On the day of her funeral, they refused to take a drink because of the love she had shown toward them. You see, on Saturdays, I remember helping my grandmother make sandwiches, take them downtown and hand them out to the street drinkers. When we drove up, you could hear them say, "Here come, Ms. Bea." No matter how hard it was for them to stand, they made an effort to do just that out of respect for this gentle woman. As she gave them one of the carefully wrapped sandwiches, she would say, "You can't drink all day and not eat." "Yes, madam," they would say. "Thank you. God bless, you Ms. Bea." In return, she would say, "God bless you. I'm praying for you and don't forget to pray too."

I remember her words, "Everybody has some good in them because God is good and everything He made is good. You just have to look harder in some people than others." She would rather build someone up than tear someone down. I saw how her soft-spoken words and ways would calm neighborhood and family situations. I saw how anger turned into soft tears at her words.

Growing up, I must say, I did not inherit that type of temperament. However, I was blessed to see it again in a young teacher as she spoke to difficult parents and students. The two of them had a way of waiting for the right moment and knowing what and how to say something to calm the situation. It was a gift of the Holy Spirit. Picture a raging bull becoming a mere mouse right in front of your eyes. It was temperament with wisdom and understanding that made situations better. One man reasoned, if he could give up drinking for a day, he might be able to do it another day. Or a parent, who tried all she could to get her child in this teacher's room, and finally accepted the child needed a special setting for behavior modifications.

God has people who He has gifted with wisdom and understanding for the teaching and leading of others. This does not mean we are not to seek wisdom and understanding for His gifts are available for the asking.

(1) Read the following two statements:

a. A wise leader must consider the situation and times.

b. Wise words must be used by wise persons to bring about wise transactions.

What are your thoughts about the statements?

_____

_____

(2) Read the following words from Mahatma Gandhi, a world leader of the 20th century (Open Mind, *Young India,* Jan. 19, 1928).

Mahatma Ghandi – Lessons from Open Mind

Keep your thoughts positive, because your thoughts become your words. Keep your behavior positive, because your behavior become your habits. Keep your habits positive, because your habits become your values. Keep your values positive, because your values become your destiny.

Truth alone will endure; all the rest will be swept away before the tide of time.

I came to the conclusion long "ago ... that all religions were true and also that all had some error in them, and whilst I hold by my own, I should hold others as dear as Hinduism. So we can only pray, if we are Hindus, not that a Christian should become a Hindu ... But our innermost prayer should be a Hindu a better Hindu, a Muslim a better Muslim, a Christian a better Christian.

What are some of your thoughts about Ghandi's "proverbial wisdom?"

_____

_____

_____

(3) Leadership Thoughts from the Late Annie T. White, a South Carolina Educator who made us laugh at ourselves (Twelve Commandments for People Who Work with People: The Chicken Little Syndrome, 1999)

Annie T. White: The Chicken Little Syndrome

Sometimes leaders are deterred from their mission because of 'The Chicken Little Syndrome." They lose faith; they decide not to start; they doubt themselves; they quit or withdraw. Anne T. White gave this advice regarding the Chicken Little Syndrome"

"To guard against that happening, you must separate your attitude from that person with the Chicken Little Syndrome. You have to say you prefer to be positive, you prefer to see the glass half full instead of half empty."

"How do you recognize people with the Chicken Little Syndrome? Listen. Their conversations will include such phrases as "It won't work here," "We've never done it that way before," "We tried that once, but it didn't work," "Let's stick to what we know."

"You have to remember, and to remind them, that if you always do what you've always done, you'll always get what you've always gotten, and sometimes that isn't good enough. Progress would not exist without someone taking risks, trying to accomplish a task in a new and better way, and it may be up to you to provide the inspiration."

"Sometimes the Chicken Little Syndrome may masquerade behind the "It's not my job" mask. It's easy to dampen team spirit by refusing to become involved in a task that is not included in your job description (Twelve Commandments for People Who Work With People, pp 46-47).

Answer the following questions:

a) Have you ever encountered the Chicken Little Syndrome?

_____

b) Have you ever been the major player in the Syndrome?

_____

c) What words of wisdom would you give yourself as to not fall prey to the Chicken Little Syndrome?

_____

(4) Oprah Winfrey - Some Thoughts on Wisdom and Life

- "Real integrity is doing the right thing, knowing that nobody's going to know whether you did it or not."

- "True forgiveness is when you can say, "Thank you for that experience."

- "You don't become what you want, you become what you believe."

- "Everyone wants to ride with you in the limo, but what you want is someone who will take the bus with you when the limo breaks down."

- "The more you praise and celebrate your life, the more there is in life to celebrate."

What are some of your thoughts about Oprah's "proverbial wisdom?"

_____

_____

_____

(5) President Barak Obama on Wisdom and Life

- "Change will not come if we wait for some other person or some other time."

- "If you're walking down the right path and you're willing to keep walking, eventually you'll make progress."

- "We need to reject any politics that targets people because of race or religion."

- "Money is not the only answer, but it makes a difference.'

What are some of your thoughts about President Obama's "proverbial wisdom?"

_____

_____

_____

(6) President Jimmy Carter, Quotes on Spiritual and Moral _Values_

- "Failure is a reality; we all fail at times, and it's painful when we do. But its's better to fail while striving for something wonderful, challenging, adventurous, and uncertain that to say, "I don't want to try because I may not succeed completely."

- Spirit is like the wind, in that we can't see it but can see its effects, which are profound."

- "God always answers prayers. Sometimes it's "yes." Sometimes the answer is "no." Sometimes it's "you gotta be kidding."

- "War may sometimes be a necessary evil. But no matter how necessary, it is always an evil, never a good. We will not learn to live together in peace by killing each other.

What are some of your thoughts about President Carter's "proverbial wisdom?"

_____

_____

_____

_____

(7) We have reflected upon thoughts of some well-known leaders in our modern world. According to Proverbs 1:5-7:

> A wise *man* will hear and increase learning,
> And a man of understanding will attain wise counsel,
> To understand a proverb and an enigma,
> The words of the wise and their riddles.

(a) How can you ensure that you have wise counsel and you are hearing from God concerning your learning?

_____

_____

(b) What are some affirmations, quotes, or Scriptures that inspire your faith walk?

_____

_____

_____

_____

(c) "When God chose you, He did not make a mistake. God chooses wisely. Failures and successes are a part of life. When we learn from our own and others' mistakes, it can make us become better Servant Leaders." *G.T. Bulluck*

What is your thought about this quote?

_____

_____

_____

_____

Psalm 139-:13-17 says,

For you created my inmost being;
  you knit me together in my mother's womb.
[14] I praise you because I am fearfully and wonderfully made;
  your works are wonderful,
  I know that full well.

[15] My frame was not hidden from you
  when I was made in the secret place,
  when I was woven together in the depths of the earth.

[16] Your eyes saw my unformed body;
  all the days ordained for me were written in your book
  before one of them came to be.

[17] How precious to me are your thoughts, God! How vast is the sum of them!

(d) What is it about God that makes you believe this is true? DON'T LIMIT YOUR THOUGHTS ABOUT HIM.

_____

_____

_____

_____

(e) Can you find a reason right NOW to praise Him?

_____

Character Traits - Takeaways

You have done quite a bit of work in Section II, Character/Traits. **Let's reflect.** You read an old tale, reviewed/researched leadership traits, reflected upon wise behaviors from Proverbs and views from world leaders. You have reflected upon your circumstances and gave responses as well. From all of this,....

What are some Key Takeaways that stood out for you? Takeaways might include anything that resonates with you. It might include experiences, challenges, loves, emotions, or changes.

Key Takeaways
You may not have key takeaways in each area.

Experience(s):

Challenge(s):

Love(s)

Emotion(s)

Change (s)

Other:

SECTION III: CHARACTER OF A LEADER

In this section, you will have the opportunity to identify character traits in some of God's chosen people for leadership (i.e., John, Saul, Deborah and Barak). From each of these characters, there is a "take-away to be learned (good or bad)."

For your convenience, most of the Scriptures referred to in the activities, have been conveniently provided in the Appendix. At the end of Section III, you will have the opportunity to assess your personal takeaway(s).

CONTENT LESSONS AND ACTIVITIES

Activity#1 The Leadership of John

Activity #2 The Leadership of Jude

Activity #3 The Leadership of Ezekiel

Activity #4 The Leadership of Moses

Activity #5 The Leadership of Saul

Activity #6 The Leadership of David

Activity #7 The Leadership of Deborah and Barak

The Leadership Model- Jesus

Activity #8 Effective Traits in Jesus

Personal Takeaway(s)

The Leadership of John

It Begins with LOVE!
"He who does not love does not know God, for God is love."
1 John 4:8 New King James Version (NKJV)

As a servant leader, John pushed the teaching doctrine of Jesus as both human and divine (1 John 5:1-5 NKJV). Apostle John is also known for his writings and teaching about 'love.' If we love another, we will help another.

"Whoever believes that Jesus is the Christ is born of God, and everyone who loves Him who begot also loves him who is begotten of Him. ² By this we know that we love the children of God, when we love God and keep His commandments. ³ For this is the love of God, that we keep His commandments. And His commandments are not burdensome. ⁴ For whatever is born of God overcomes the world. And this is the victory that has overcome the world—our faith. ⁵ Who is he who overcomes the world, but he who believes that Jesus is the Son of God?"

Activity #1 Leadership of John

(1) Read the letter 3 John Chapter 1 (Appendix) written from Apostle John to Gaius, of Ephesus, a church leader.

(2) Examine the characteristics of the leaders mentioned in this Scripture. Referring to the characteristics or principles found in "Character Traits in Proverbs Chart 2," identify a trait and reference the Scripture for:

(a) Apostle John

Trait: _____

Scripture: _____

(b) Gaius (house-church leader)

Trait: _____

Scripture: _____

(c) Diotrephes (another house-church leader)

Trait: _____

Scripture: _____

(d) Demetrius (sent by Apostle John)

Trait: _____

Scripture: _____

(3) What characteristics do you believe the Scripture expose as harmful?

_____

(4) What characteristics do you believe the Scripture expose as most charitable?

_____

(5) Can you think of a situation where either characteristic would serve you well or bring dishonor to leadership?

_____

The Leadership of Jude

(a servant of Jesus Christ and brother of James, the son of Joseph)

> *"We cannot be an encouragement if we live our lives in secret caves, pushing people away from us. People out of touch don't encourage others. Encouragement is a face-to-face thing."*
>
> *Growing Deep in the Christian Life, .375*

Activity #2 The Leadership of Jude

(1) Read *the letter of Jude* (in the Appendix).

(2) Answer the following questions.

    (a) What are the characteristics of the ungodly leaders described in verses 1-19?

_____

_____

_____

    (b) What characteristics are godly leaders called to demonstrate in verses 20-23?

_____

_____

    (c) What are the descriptions of God in verse 24?

_____

_____

_____

    (d) What format could you use to encourage people to emerge themselves in their calling or gifts? Reflect upon Jude and the statement "Encouragement is a face-to-face thing."

_____

_____

_____

The Leadership of Ezekiel

"Those who know your name will trust in you, for you, Lord, have never forsaken those who seek you. Psalm 9:10 NIV

Selective deportations were a common practice among warring nations during ancient and Biblical times. The removal of political, financial and spiritual leaders was meant to defuse a nation's resistance against the conquering nation. Ezekiel (as Isaiah and Jeremiah) was a prophetic leader during such times. God spoke to him and gave him understanding of objects in a divine spiritual manner to foretell and describe future events pertaining to nations and kings, e.g., Israel, Nebuchadnezzar, Philistia, etc. Ezekiel spoke in a manner, "Thus says the Lord," and "The word of the Lord came to me."

Activity #3 The Leadership of Ezekiel

(1) Ezekiel 33:7, Called again to be a Watchman - Read Ezekiel 33:1-9 (Appendix). Ezekiel's role as a watchman was a divine calling by God. The job of the watchman was to strategically stand at a place where he could view the approaching enemy and warn the people of the enemy's approach. Ezekiel's job was to warn the people to heed and be obedient to God.

As a servant leader, what traits would you choose to avoid as a watchman in the support of ministry? Use Chart 2, Character Traits in Proverbs, to help you with your answer.

_____

_____

_____

_____

(2) Ezekiel 2:1-3; Called to be a Prophet

He said to me, "Son of man, stand up on your feet and I will speak to you." [2] As he spoke, the Spirit came into me and raised me to my feet, and I heard him speaking to me.

[3] He said: "Son of man, I am sending you to the Israelites, to a rebellious nation that has rebelled against me; they and their ancestors have been in revolt against me to this very day.

In the following verses of Chapter 2, God compels Ezekiel to *not be afraid, listen to Him and speak His word*s.

From Chart 2, what traits do you believe are essential to your leadership under similar conditions?

_____

_____

(3) Ezekiel, The Anointed Visionary - Read Ezekiel 1:1-22 (Appendix).

Ezekiel's vision in chapter 1 is a symbolic representation or imagery (a wheel in the middle of a wheel). As a servant leader, use the imagery of a "wheel in the middle of a wheel" and answer the following questions.

According to Ezekiel 1, verse 18, all four rims were full of eyes. "Full eyes" mean divine eyes.

(a) How can you keep your eyes divine? Refer to Chart 2, Character Traits in Proverbs, to support your answer. Identify a trait to promote and/or avoid.

_____

_____

_____

(b) According to Ezekiel 1:20, there was eye to eye agreement. How can you operate as a servant leader to ensure eye to eye in ministry? Your answer must be based on Scripture and not personal thoughts. Use Chart 2 or another Scripture to support your answer.

_____

_____

_____

(4) According to Ezekiel 1:22, there was a likeness of the firmament above the heads of the living creatures like the color of an awesome crystal. We know shining crystals _sparkles_. The verse states that the image was stretched out over their heads. This seems to suggest a covering that sparkled and stretched over. The definition of firmament is something like a vault, a covering. In the spiritual realm, the object can be representative of leadership support.

(a) How can you as a leader be a "pillar" holding up the Church according to The Word of God. Use Chart 2 or reference another Scripture.

_____

_____

_____

_____

(b) Read Hebrews 13:13-18 from your Bible.

How do these verses identify or characterize leaders as "pillars of support to the Church?"

Verse 15:

_____

_____

_____

_____

Verse 17:

_____

_____

_____

_____

Verse 18:

_____

_____

_____

_____

(5) The imagery was also of a chariot with wheels facing all four directions – East, West, North, South. In the natural, such a wheel COULD NOT effectively move in the same direction. However, in the spiritual realm, this imagery can symbolize the relationship between the pastor and leaders in the church? How could leaders ensure that the inner wheel moves with the outer wheel? Your answer must be scripturally sound.

_____

_____

_____

(6) Read Ezekiel 4:1-8 (Appendix).

As we have noted, leadership will come under siege. Siege warfare was a common practice in ancient and Biblical times. A siege is a military blockade of a city, or fortress, with the intent of conquering by a well-prepared assault. Sieges involved surrounding the targeted nation to block the provision of supplies, reinforcement or escape. This passage deals with the prophecy of Jerusalem under siege.

In what ways, does your leadership or some other leadership come under siege?

_____

_____

_____

(7) God has given us a protective armor against reoccurring sieges (Ephesians 6:10-12). We wrestle not against flesh and blood.

Read Ephesians 6:14-20 (Appendix). Write out these directives or instructions on a separate piece of paper. Post or keep them in a place for constant viewing, asking God's protection.

_____

_____

_____

_____

The Leadership of Moses

> *From everlasting to everlasting the Lord's love is with those who fear him,*
> *and his righteousness with their children's children. Psalm 103:17 NIV*

Activity #4 The Leadership of Moses

Read the following passage:

"So, Moses' father-in-law said to him, "The thing that you do is not good. Both you and these people who are with you will surely wear yourselves out. For this thing is too much for you; you are not able to perform it by yourself. Listen now to my voice; I will give you counsel, and God will be with you: Stand before God for the people, so that you may bring the difficulties to God," Exodus 18:17-19 NKJV.

Leadership can be exhausting. The body and mind needs refreshing so that you are prepared to hear in the spiritual realm. What are regularly refreshing ways you implement so you are prepared for spending time with God and developing your relationship with Him?

_____

_____

_____

_____

Use Chart 2 "Character Traits Found in Proverbs" to answer the next two questions.

(1) What leadership characteristic(s) does Jethro (the father-in-law of Moses and Priest of Midian) exhibit based on the proverbial traits listed?

_____

_____

_____

_____

(2) What leadership characteristic(s) does Moses exhibit based on the proverbial traits listed?

_____

_____

_____

_____

(3) Read the following verses: "And *you shall teach them the statutes and the laws and show them the way in which they must walk and the work they must do. Moreover, you shall select from all the people able men, such as fear God, men of truth, hating covetousness; (vv 20-21).*

What leadership actions does Jethro announce in verses 20-21?

_____

_____

_____

_____

(4) Read the following from Acts 6:3-4. *"Therefore, brethren, seek out from among you seven men of good reputation, full of the Holy Spirit and wisdom, whom we may appoint over this business; but we will give ourselves continually to prayer and to the ministry of the word."*

As with Moses, the disciples needed others to work in the ministry of Helps.

Identify the traits of the leaders listed in Acts 6:3-4.

_____

_____

_____

_____

(5) As a servant leader, how do you view your role as a part of the HELPS ministry (if at all).

_____

_____

A Perspective of the Leadership of Moses

"A servant leader must not forget that leadership is for the Kingdom of God."

The leadership of Moses has served as an example to a countless number of leaders. His calling was from God (Exodus 3:1-12). When Moses was called to lead, the Scripture tells us that he was not over-joyed for several reasons (after-all, he had murdered an Egyptian soldier). Moses also felt inadequate to lead because of a speech impediment. But his reason should be a reminder that whatever our imperfections, God is our strength – Our Source – Our El Shaddai. Knowing this should give us comfort; relieve some of the anxiety that many of us still feel; and aid us in stepping up to our call; for God is able and willing to provide the resources for our assignments (God even sent Aaron as a support to Moses).

However, let us keep in mind that Moses was the designated leader for the completion of the assigned purpose - lead the children of Israel out of slavery into the Promise Land. It was Moses who was given the Law of God for the people of God (Exodus 20). It was Moses whom God met face-to-face. It was Moses who performed miraculous signs in the presence of the people. He was an imperfect man called by the perfect God.

God knows our fragilities. Moses was not infallible and the Bible records how Moses failed to follow God's instructions (in Numbers 20:10-12, Deuteronomy 32:51-52, and Exodus 17). In fact, Aaron and Moses were not allowed to enter the Promise Land because of disobedience. The result of their disobedience cost them greatly, even though, God was merciful and allowed Moses to view the Promise Land.

This brings us to the reasoning of "follow-through is essential in leadership." Passing the assignment on to someone else should only be done with the approval of God. Doing so outside of the authorization will cause harm. Moses finally recognized this and shared what he had learned before his leaving "the stage." His message was to remind them that they are God's people, move forward and complete the assignment knowing that God is with you. "For Moses truly said to the fathers, 'The LORD your God will raise up for you a Prophet like me from your brethren. Him you shall hear in all things, whatever He says to you. And it shall be *that* every soul who will not hear that Prophet shall be utterly destroyed from among the people.' Yes, and all the prophets, from Samuel and those who follow, as many as have spoken, have also foretold these days. You are sons of the prophets, and of the covenant which God made with our fathers, saying to Abraham, 'And in your seed all the families of the earth shall be blessed," Acts 3:22-25.

Moses' call was to that of a NEED. Too often, leaders equate service to that of pleasing God. But pleasing God comes through the fulfilling of a NEED. The very reason that Jesus came was because of a NEED. Our salvation depended upon His Works. We had need of Him. "To you first, God, having raised up His Servant Jesus, sent Him to bless you, in turning away every one *of you* from your iniquities," Acts 3:26. God gives assignments because there is a need. Jesus said he came to heal. A physician is not needed for the healthy person. The physician is sent to the sick. It is cowardly, hurtful and counterfeit to serve without love and recognition of that NEED. Jesus addressed the needs of people; His focus was NEED. " For He had to go through Samaria," John 4:4. Why? Because there was Samaritan woman who had need of Him.

Stepping up your call to Servant Leadership NOW means you have to go through Samaria. We must understand that servant leadership is about addressing the NEED of those we serve; otherwise your service is counterproductive. And counterfeit service will burn up as chaff.

BUT - How rewarding it is to be obedient to God for the Kingdom. He promises everlasting life.

The Leadership Of Saul

Power, Position and Personality

> Then Samuel took a flask of oil and poured it on his head, and kissed him and said; "Is it not because the lord has anointed you commander over his inheritance.' 1 Samuel 10:1 NKJV

Activity #5 The Leadership of Saul

Power, Position and Personality! The Book of Samuel includes the narrative story of two contrasting figures who played a significant leadership role after the exodus of the Israelites from Egypt - Saul and David. As prophesied by prophets like Isaiah, Jerimiah, and Samuel, the children of Israel would suffer because of their disobedience to God. In the following reading assignments, you will identify leadership traits of these two leaders from the prospective of **position, power and character (personality)** and relate some of these attributes to your personal leadership style.

ILL-GOTTEN!

Ill-gotten position and power will cause devastation. A servant leader's character and relationship with God is essential to one's personal successes and failures. People will examine leaders by their successes and failures; they want leaders to show a history of success. But ill-gotten success is not real success. **Real servant leaders of God must draw from the "well" of God for real success.** They must look to God for directions and decision-making to be successful in their leadership. This is where real power descends.

Saul is an example of ill-gotten position and power by a leader. The children of Israel were impressed by his statute. They desired his leadership, even if it was ill-gotten. He was not the anointed by God. It was their indifferences and refusal to wait on God which cost them a better life as a nation and community.

Unfortunately, many people are impressed by the personality of leaders and not their relationship with God. Perhaps more than we like to admit, people are accepting of superficial leadership for their own personal gain. Adhering to God's agenda is inconceivable if it gets in the way of their personal wants. The result can be devastating. When leadership is at odds with God's agenda, tragedy awaits.

Let's take a closer look at the leadership of Saul and David in the next pages.

(1) Remind yourself of the beginning relationship of David and Saul in 1 Samuel 17. Verses from 1 Samuel 17:32-33, 38-40,45,50 are listed for background scriptural review in the Appendix.

(2) Read 1 Samuel 18:1-16 about the resentment of Saul, and the relationship of David and Jonathan (Appendix).

(a) What is Saul's leadership position? What is David's leadership position? Who is Jonathan?

Saul _____

David _____

Jonathan _____

(b) What traits are to be promoted or traits to be avoided? What character traits of Saul are on display in verses 8-13?

_____

_____

_____

_____

(3) Read 1 Samuel 18:17-29 (Appendix).
Again, whether traits are to be promoted or avoided, what character traits of Saul are on display:

In verses 17-22?

_____

_____

_____

_____

In verse 25?

_____

_____

_____

_____

(4) Read 1 Samuel 19:1-17 (Appendix).

In this chapter, Jonathan and Michael act as intercessors. As a servant leader, what character traits do you view as necessary? You may refer to Chart 2, Character Traits in Proverbs.

_____

_____

_____

_____

(5) Read 1 Samuel 19:18-24 about the Interceding of The Spirit of God.

Samuel and the prophets interceded on behalf of David. The Spirit of God came upon the messengers of Saul (three times), and they also prophesied. The Spirit of God took hold of Saul and he prophesied. As a servant leader, what can be gleaned about the power of the Holy Spirit in leadership?

_____

_____

_____

_____

(6) Read 1 Samuel 20 (Appendix). What personality (character traits) are operating in this instance that a servant leader should avoid? Refer to Chart 2 as a reference in support of your answer.

_____

_____

_____

(7) Read 1 Samuel 22 (Appendix). Saul uses his power and position in dealing with Ahimelech and the priests of Nob including the destruction of people of the city. "Also Nob, the city of the priests, he struck with the edge of the sword, both men and women, children and nursing infants, oxen and donkeys and sheep—with the edge of the sword (verse 19)."

What is the personality (character traits) operating, in this instance, that a servant leader should avoid?

_____

_____

_____

_____

(8) As a Bible student, how did the calling of Saul differ from the calling of David? Refer to 1 Samuel 9 and 2 Samuel 5.

_____

_____

_____

_____

Power, Position and Personality

The Leadership of David

> But the LORD said to Samuel, "Do not look at his appearance or at his physical stature, because I have refused him. For[d] *the LORD does* not *see* as man sees; for man looks at the outward appearance, but the LORD looks at the heart." 1 Samuel 16:7 NKJV

Activity #6 The Leadership of David

David, as God's anointed leader of Israel, made his mistakes. He possessed both **power** and **position** as a leader. At times, he was at odds with the will of God (1 Samuel 25:23-31; 2 Samuel 11). Through his journey, we encounter David as a more astute (wise) leader as he strengthened his relationship with God. Servant Leadership demands that leaders are nurturing, wise and faithful in carrying out the will of God.

(1) Read this prayer of David from Psalm 86 NKJV.

1 *Bow* down Your ear, O LORD, hear me; For I *am* poor and needy.

2 Preserve my life, for I *am* holy; You are my God; Save Your servant who trusts in You!

3 Be merciful to me, O Lord, For I cry to You all day long.

4 Rejoice the soul of Your servant, For to You, O Lord, I lift up my soul.

5 For You, Lord, *are* good, and ready to forgive, And abundant in mercy to all those who call upon You.

6 Give ear, O LORD, to my prayer; And attend to the voice of my supplications.

7 In the day of my trouble I will call upon You, For You will answer me.

8 Among the gods *there is* none like You, O Lord; Nor *are there any works* like Your works.

9 All nations whom You have made Shall come and worship before You, O Lord,
And shall glorify Your name.

10 For You *are* great, and do wondrous things; You alone *are* God.

11 Teach me Your way, O LORD; I will walk in Your truth; Unite my heart to fear Your name.

12 I will praise You, O Lord my God, with all my heart, And I will glorify Your name forevermore.

13 For great *is* Your mercy toward me, And You have delivered my soul from the depths of Sheol.

14 O God, the proud have risen against me, And a mob of violent *men* have sought my life, And have not set You before them.

15 But You, O Lord, *are* a God full of compassion, and gracious, Longsuffering and abundant in mercy and truth.

16 Oh, turn to me, and have mercy on me! Give Your strength to Your servant,
And save the son of Your maidservant.

17 Show me a sign for good, That those who hate me may see *it* and be ashamed, Because You, Lord, have helped me and comforted me.

(2) Read 1 Samuel 21 (Appendix).

In this text, we see David on the run from Saul. It is evident that David deceived his enemies to protect his life. In Nob, he saw the fear of Ahimelech and lied about his reasons for being in Nob. Several theories have been suggested as to why David lied to the priest Ahimelech. To Achish, the king of Gath, he pretended to be a mad man. In the culture of the Philistines, madness was an affliction caused by a god. A prophet who is possessed by a god, could live and would be turned out of the city from among the people. David's decisions, whether to protect Ahimelech or himself, cannot be blamed for the action of Saul, his enemy.

(a) As a servant leader, you are responsible for your own responses to situations. What character traits do you desire to promote over others or choose to avoid?

_____

_____

_____

_____

(b) How can the Holy Spirit support a servant leader in decision-making? What Scripture(s) supports your answer?

_____

_____

_____

(3) Read 1 Samuel 22 (Appendix).

(a) In verses 1-5, what character trait(s) of David's are evident?

_____

_____

_____

_____

(b) In verses 20-23, David reacts to the killing of the priests and people of Nod. As a servant leader, what steps does David take as an intercessor? What character traits are evident? Use Chart 2 as a supporting tool to your answer.

_____

_____

_____

_____

(4) Read 1 Samuel 23 (Appendix).

As a servant leader, what is the wisdom of David on display:
(a) In verses 1-4?

_____

_____

_____

_____

(b) In verses 9-12?

_____

_____

_____

_____

(5) Read 1 Samuel 23:13-18 (Appendix).

"Then Jonathan, Saul's son, arose and went to David in the woods and strengthened his hand in God (verse 16)." How can an intercessor as Jonathan be important to leadership in carrying out God's agenda? Use Chart 2, if needed.

_____

_____

_____

_____

(6) Read 1 Samuel 23:19-23.

While Saul was pursuing David, the Philistines invaded the land of Israel, ("Hurry and come, for the Philistines have invaded the land"). David called the place where Saul left off in pursuit, the Rock of Escape.

(a) As a servant leader, what does this say about God?

_____

_____

_____

_____

(b) How has God been your 'Rock of Escape'?

_____

_____

_____

_____

(7) Read 1 Samuel 24 (Appendix).

Use Chart 2, and contrast the character traits of David and Saul. How do they differ?

David's Traits	Saul's Traits

(8) Read 1 Samuel 25 (Appendix).

David's leadership was continually opposed and tested. However, David understood that he was orchestrating God's agenda.

Use Chart 2; contrast the character traits of David and Nabal. How do they differ?

David's Traits	Nabal's Traits

(9) Again, we see God has provided an intercessor. Let's think about who is the intercessor and what character traits does the intercessor display?

"…And she was a woman of good understanding and beautiful appearance; but the man was harsh and evil in his doings. He was of the house of Caleb."

Intercessor's Name:

_____

_____

Character Traits:

_____

_____

_____

(10) Read verses 32-25. What traits are identifiable in David's response to this intercessor.

_____

_____

_____

_____

Identifiable Character Traits in Response to Abigail are:

_____

_____

_____

_____

(11) Consider verse 39; "So when David heard that Nabal was dead, he said, "Blessed *be* the Lord, who has pleaded the cause of my reproach from the hand of Nabal, and has kept His servant from evil! For the Lord has returned the wickedness of Nabal on his own head."

Once again, God has provided protection to David, saving him from himself.

(a) As a servant leader, how has God provided protection for you, saving you from yourself?

_____

_____

(b) Based on God's Word, how do you know God will provide protection to his children?

Research a Scripture(s) that gives you assurance.
Scripture:

_____

_____

_____

_____

_____

(12) Read 1 Samuel 26: 9-11, reads, "But David said to Abishai, "Do not destroy him; for who can stretch out his hand against the LORD's anointed, and be guiltless?" [10] David said furthermore, "*As* the LORD lives, the LORD shall strike him, or his day shall come to die, or he shall go out to battle and perish. [11] The LORD forbid that I should stretch out my hand against the LORD's anointed.

In Psalm 86, David prayed for God's mercy on his leadership. "Show me a sign for good, that those who hate me may see *it* and be ashamed, Because You, LORD, have helped me and comforted me (verse 17)."

As a servant leader, you are called to walk in obedience so that God can bless your leadership. David prayed in sincerity in carrying out God's agenda. He understood that he needed God's divine protection. His prayers were not in conflict with God's purpose for his life. What is your prayer to God for protection and guidance in leading others?

_____

_____

_____

_____

(13) Read 1 Samuel 26:8-12 (Appendix).

Contrast David and Abishai as servant leaders. Use Chart 2 to support your answer.

David's Traits	Abishai's Traits

Note: Saul killed the father of Abishai (1 Samuel 22:16-20).

(14) Read 1 Samuel 30.

While David and his soldiers were fighting the Amalekites, another enemy kept into his camp, took advantage of their being away and captured their city and took their families. Verse 6 states, "Now David was greatly distressed, for the people spoke of stoning him, because the soul of all the people was grieved, every man for his sons and his daughters. But David strengthened himself in the Lord his God."

(a) In leadership, how do you seek the Lord and strengthen yourself?

_____

_____

_____

_____

_____

(b) What Scriptures do you have as an assurance that God will answer?

_____

_____

_____

_____

(c) In verses 21-25 of the Scripture, David uses his power, position and character to lead the people in the way of the Lord regarding fairness. "So it was, from that day forward; he made it a statute and an ordinance for Israel to this day."

If God dealt fairly with you, what would be the result? What would be the result of power, position and character?

_____

_____

_____

_____

(d) David prayed in Psalm 86:3-5:

Be merciful to me, O Lord, For I cry to You all day long.

Rejoice the soul of Your servant, For to You, O Lord, I lift up my soul. For You, Lord, are good, and ready to forgive, And abundant in mercy to all those who call upon You.

In leadership, how have you demonstrated the mercy of the Lord in someone else's life?

_____

_____

_____

_____

(e) In 1 Samuel 24:14-22, we read how David demonstrated mercy and kindness toward Saul, and even spared Saul's life. How does the mercy and kindness of God toward you resemble the mercy and kindness of David?

_____

_____

_____

_____

(f) Read 2 Samuel 9:1-13.
Keeping his promise to Saul, "Therefore swear now to me by the Lord that you will not cut off my descendants after me, and that you will not destroy my name from my father's house, (I Samuel 24:21)," David showed graciousness to Jonathan, Saul's son.

David prayed in Psalm 86:13-15

For great *is* Your mercy toward me,
And You have delivered my soul from the depths of Sheol.
O God, the proud have risen against me,
And a mob of violent *men* have sought my life,
And have not set You before them.
But You, O Lord, *are* a God full of compassion, and gracious,
Longsuffering and abundant in mercy and truth.

David's graciousness was more than just symbolic; it was in deed and word (tangible).

How does God show *compassion, gracious, longsuffering and abundant in mercy and truth?* How has His attributes helped you in leadership?

_____

_____

(15) Read 2 Samuel 12:1-10 how **Nathan Rebukes David** for his sin.
    What are your thoughts concerning David's position, power and personality?

_____

_____

(16) Read 2 Samuel 16:1-4; Reciprocation of kindness.

What are your thoughts about Ziba's actions?

_____

_____

_____

(17) What is the opposite action of kindness? _____

What could be the effects of this action?

_____

_____

Reread Proverbs 11:16-17 concerning kindness. _____

Write out a verse(s) from Proverbs 25:21-22 that you find helpful in your leadership.

_____

_____

_____

_____

_____

_____

_____

_____

The Leadership of Deborah and Barak

Servant Leadership is based on trust in God; it is the core principle of developing a relationship with Him.

Activity #7 The Leadership of Deborah and Barak

(1) Read Judges 4:1-10 (Appendix).

(2) Answer the following questions.

    a. What verses demonstrate Barak's refusal or hesitation to lead Israel in battle?

_____

_____

_____

_____

    b. What verses demonstrate in whom Barak placed his trust?

_____

_____

_____

_____

    c. Deborah was a wife, a judge of Israel and a prophetess. What verses in this chapter and in Judges chapter 5 demonstrate her wisdom and trust in God?

_____

_____

_____

_____

_____

_____

The Leadership Model - Jesus

"God's presence is evident in the life of an effective Leader."

"For God so loved the world that He gave His only begotten Son, that whoever believes in Him should not perish but have everlasting life," John 3:16 NKJV.

"But when the fullness of the time had come, God sent forth His Son, born of a woman, born under the law, to redeem those who were under the law, that we might receive the adoption as sons," Galatians 4:4-5 NKJV.

Jesus is our model of leadership. His leadership was based on his **Father's will (God's agenda)**. Whether listening, teaching, praying, preaching, or performing miracles, he knew the assignment given to him was from the Father. Affirming his calling to carryout God's plan, he stated: *"I can of Myself do nothing. As I hear, I judge; and My judgment is righteous, because I do not seek My own will but the will of the Father who sent Me," John 5:30.*

There are certain characteristics i.e., wisdom, prayer, fasting, faith, mentoring, holiness, and obedience to God, which stand out in Jesus's modeled service:

As a servant leader, Jesus grew in **wisdom** and stature. When he became of age, he began to be about his Father's business. *"Every year Jesus' parents went to Jerusalem for the Festival of the Passover. When he was twelve years old, they went up to the festival, according to the custom. After three days they found him in the temple courts, sitting among the teachers, listening to them and asking them questions. Everyone who heard him was amazed at his understanding and his answers," Luke 2, 41, 42, 46, and 47.* To his earthly parents, *"And He said to them, "Why did you seek Me? Did you not know that I must be about My Father's business?" Luke 2:49.*

As a servant leader, Jesus was always **obedient to God**. Examples of such obedience was demonstrated in the wilderness and in the Garden (at the Mount of Olives). *"When He had been baptized, Jesus came up immediately from the water; and behold, the heavens were opened to Him, and He saw the Spirit of God descending like a dove and alighting upon Him. And suddenly a voice came from heaven, saying, "This is My beloved Son, in whom I am well pleased," Matthew 3:16-17. "Immediately the Spirit drove Him into the wilderness. And He was there in the wilderness forty days, tempted by Satan, and was with the wild beasts; and the angels ministered to Him," Mark 1:12.* In the Mount of Olives, *"And He was withdrawn from them about a stone's throw, and He knelt down and prayed, saying, "Father, if it is Your will, take this cup away from Me; nevertheless not My will, but Yours, be done." Then an angel appeared to Him from heaven, strengthening Him. And being in agony, He prayed more earnestly. Then His sweat became like great drops of blood falling down to the ground," Luke 22:41-44.*

God honored Jesus's obedience with strength and power to overcome evil. His spirit was renewed to carry-out his assignment.

As a servant leader, when the season of time came, by wisdom and in obedience, Jesus called and **mentored** twelve chosen disciples, *"Come, follow me," Jesus said, "and I will send you out to fish for people," Mark 1:17. "Now it came to pass in those days that He went out to the mountain to pray, and continued all night in prayer to God. And when it was day, He called His disciples to Himself; and from them He chose twelve whom He also named apostles: Simon, whom He also named Peter, and Andrew his brother; James and John; Philip and Bartholomew; Matthew and Thomas; James the son of Alphaeus, and Simon called the Zealot; Judas the son of James, and Judas Iscariot who also became a traitor," Luke 6:12-17. "While I was with them in the world, I kept them in Your name. Those whom You gave Me I have kept; and none of them is lost except the son of perdition, that the Scripture might be fulfilled," (John 17:12).*

As their mentor, Jesus did not misuse **power, position, or authority.** Rather he demonstrated how to use what God has given to bring people to God. *"The people were all so amazed that they asked each other, "What is this? A new teaching—and with authority! He even gives orders to impure spirits and they obey him,"* (Mark 1:27).

As a leader, Jesus knew the importance and power of **prayer** in his relationship with His Heavenly Father. Prayer amplified his relationship with God. The Bible speaks of Jesus constant praying in solitude for direction. *"Now in the morning, having risen a long while before daylight, He went out and departed to a solitary place; and there He prayed.," (v. 35).* He taught his disciples about solitude and sincerity of prayer. *"And when you pray, you shall not be like the hypocrites. For they love to pray standing in the synagogues and on the corners of the streets, that they may be seen by men. Assuredly, I say to you, they have their reward. But you, when you pray, go into your room, and when you have shut your door, pray to your Father who is in the secret place; and your Father who sees in secret will reward you openly. And when you pray, do not use vain repetitions as the heathen do. For they think that they will be heard for their many words," Matthew 6:5-7.*

He taught them that some things come with fasting as well as prayer; and have faith in God when you pray. *"So, Jesus said to them, "Because of your unbelief; for assuredly, I say to you, if you have faith as a mustard seed, you will say to this mountain, 'Move from here to there,' and it will move; and nothing will be impossible for you. However, this kind does not go out except by prayer and fasting," Matthew 17:20-21.* Listen to hear His voice.

Jesus was consistent in praying for his followers. *"I do not pray that You should take them out of the world, but that You should keep them from the evil one. They are not of the world, just as I am not of the world. Sanctify them by Your truth. Your word is truth. As You sent Me into the world, I also have sent them into the world. And for their sakes I sanctify Myself, that they also may be sanctified by the truth.," John 17:15-19. "I do not pray for these alone, but also for those who will believe in Me through their word; that they all may be one, as You, Father, are in Me, and I in You; that they also may be one in Us, that the world may believe that You sent Me.," (John 17:20-21).*

In prayer, the Holy Spirit is willing to cooperate with you. The Holy Spirit will lead you. The following passage of Scripture is an example. The disciples were anxious for Jesus to come back and speak to people. But after prayer, Jesus followed the direction of His Father and went forward to the next towns to preach. *"When they found Him, they said to Him, "Everyone is looking for You." But He said to them, "Let us go into the next towns, that I may preach there also, because for this purpose I have come forth," (Mark 1: 37-38).* Expect God to answer.

As a servant leader, Jesus sought to please the Father. Jesus understood that God is to be glorified. He glorified **the Father** even unto death. *Jesus spoke these words, lifted up His eyes to heaven, and said: "Father, the hour has come. Glorify Your Son, that Your Son also may glorify You, as You have given Him authority over all flesh, that He should give eternal life to as many as You have given Him. And this is eternal life, that they may know You, the only true God, and Jesus Christ whom You have sent. I have glorified You on the earth. I have finished the work which You have given Me to do. And now, O Father, glorify Me together with Yourself, with the glory which I had with You before the world was. how to glorify His Father,"*
John 17:1-5.

Acting with wisdom and obedience to God, as a leader, he mentored and lead a prayerful life - giving God all the glory. What a leadership model!

Activity #8 Effective Leadership Traits in Jesus

In this activity, we noted Scripture that identify effective traits operating in Jesus. However, there are others as well.

Research another Scripture which portrays Jesus, our model leader, demonstrating at least one of these traits.

Jesus, Our Model Leader

Trait	Scripture Example	Your Scripture Example
Faith/Trust	Matthew 26:39, "He went a little farther and fell on His face, and prayed, saying, "O My Father, if it is possible, let this cup pass from Me; nevertheless, not as I will, but as You will,"	
Holy Spirit/ God's Presence	Mark 9:7-8, "And a cloud came and overshadowed them; and a voice came out of the cloud, saying, "This is My beloved Son. Hear Him!" Suddenly, when they had looked around, they saw no one anymore, but only Jesus with themselves.	
Integrity (Honesty, Truthfulness)	John 10:25, Jesus answered them, "I told you, and you do not believe. The works that I do in My Father's name, they bear witness of Me."	
Love	John 10:11, "I am the good shepherd. The good shepherd gives His life for the sheep."	

Preparation	Mark 1:15, and saying, "The time is fulfilled, and the kingdom of God is at hand. Repent, and believe in the gospel."	
Service/Serve	John 13:8, "Peter said to Him, "You shall never wash my feet!" Jesus answered him, "If I do not wash you, you have no part with Me,"	
Prayerful	Luke 6:12, "Now it came to pass in those days that He went out to the mountain to pray, and continued all night in prayer to God,"	

Character of a Leader Takeaways

"What are some Key Takeaways for you?" Takeaways might include anything that resonates with you. It might include *experiences, challenges, loves, emotions, or changes based on the leadership style of biblical character(s). It might include a Scripture.*

Your Takeaways

Experience(s):

Challenge(s)

Love(s)

Emotion(s)

Change(s)

Other:

SECTION IV: RESPONSIBLE SERVANT LEADERSHIP

In this section, you will have the opportunity to read about and review Scriptures concerning the rewards, influences and consequences of Servant leadership. Specifically, lessons and activities will focus on personal responsibility of servant leaders according to The Word of God.

CONTENT LESSONS AND ACTIVITIES

Obedience The Great Influencer
- ❖ Activity #1A – Obedience: The Servant's Influencer
- ❖ Activity #1B - Obedience: Warnings and Benefits

Warnings Against False Teachings and Deception: Avoiding Cult or Elitist Influences
- ❖ Activity #2 – Required Service that Pleases God
- ❖ Activity #3 – Contend for the Faith

Required Forgiveness in Servant leadership
- ❖ Activity #4 – Forgiveness versus Unforgiveness
- ❖ Activity #5 - Be-in-Attitude
- ❖ Activity #6 - Father, Forgive Them

Personal Takeaways

Obedience The Great Influencer

Obedience to God is a great influencer. Through obedience, Jesus influenced and led. He did NOT teach one way and lead another way. To identify one's self as a Christian says that you are a follower of Christ. The result of Jesus the Christ's obedience to the Father is our salvation. Jesus said his children knows his voice. This means that servant leaders will aim to be obedient for God knows the way we should go.

An example of a leader who thought he was on God's agenda but was not Saul. "Now the word of the Lord came to Samuel, saying, "I greatly regret that I have set up Saul *as* king, for he has turned back from following Me, and has not performed My commandments," I Samuel 10:11 NKJV.

> [20] And Saul said to Samuel, "But I have obeyed the voice of the Lord, and gone on the mission on which the Lord sent me, and brought back Agag king of Amalek; I have utterly destroyed the Amalekites. [21] But the people took of the plunder, sheep and oxen, the best of the things which should have been utterly destroyed, to sacrifice to the Lord your God in Gilgal." I Samuel 15:20-21 NKJV. So Samuel said: "Has the Lord *as great* delight in burnt offerings and sacrifices, As in obeying the voice of the Lord? Behold, to obey is better than sacrifice, *And* to heed than the fat of rams. For rebellion *is as* the sin of witchcraft, And stubbornness *is as* iniquity and idolatry. Because you have rejected the word of the Lord, He also has rejected you from *being* king," I Samuel 15:22-23 NKJV.

An example of a leader who served and obeyed the voice of God was Job. Job's leadership was that of a righteous leader who honored God in service. And God rewarded Job for leading by obedience and not by personal influence or people standards.

We should be able to agree, based on the Scriptures, that just because a person is in a leadership position, it does not mean that the person is led by the Holy Spirit or appointed by God. Jesus taught that those who are led by him (and the person of the Holy Spirit) will walk in godliness, teach sound doctrine, produce good works and avoid corruptness. Knowledge of the truth that leads to **godliness**. Paul furthered this teaching as essential to the faith (Titus 1). Such are those who qualify for leadership.

"He who follows righteousness and mercy, Finds life, righteousness and honor," Proverbs 21:21 NKJV. Leadership that blesses the people and honor God comes through obedience to God.

Activity #1A Obedience: The Servant's Influencer

(1) The first obligation of servant leaders is to God. Love God above all. Read Matthew 23:37-40 below:

> [37]Jesus said to him, "'You shall love the Lord your God with all your heart, with all your soul, and with all your mind.' [38] This is *the* first and great commandment. [39] And *the* second *is* like it: 'You shall love your neighbor as yourself.' [40] On these two commandments hang all the Law and the Prophets."

How does this Scripture influence one's leadership style or servant leadership?

_____

_____

_____

_____

(2) Read the following Scripture: "If the Lord delights in a man's way, he will not fall, for the Lord upholds him with his hand," Psalm 37:23-24 NIV.

What evidence from the Scriptures can you offer that support the above statement as a true doctrine?

_____

_____

_____

_____

How does this Scripture influence your leadership as a servant?

_____

_____

_____

_____

(3) According to Matthew 6:1-4 NKJV, "*Take heed that you do not do your charitable deeds before men, to be seen by them. Otherwise you have no reward from your Father in heaven. [2] Therefore,*

when you do a charitable deed, do not sound a trumpet before you as the hypocrites do in the synagogues and in the streets, that they may have glory from men. Assuredly, I say to you, they have their reward. ³ But when you do a charitable deed, do not let your left hand know what your right hand is doing, ⁴ that your charitable deed may be in secret; and your Father who sees in secret will Himself reward you openly."

(a) What evidence from the Scriptures can you offer in support of this Scripture verse as sound doctrine?

_____

_____

_____

_____

(b) What impact does the Scriptures have on your personal leadership as a servant?

_____

_____

_____

_____

According to Titus 3:1-11(NIV),

¹Remind the people to be subject to rulers and authorities, to be obedient, to be ready to do whatever is good, ²to slander no one, to be peaceable and considerate, and always to be gentle toward everyone. ³At one time we too were foolish, disobedient, deceived and enslaved by all kinds of passions and pleasures. We lived in malice and envy, being hated and hating one another. ⁴But when the kindness and love of God our Savior appeared, ⁵he saved us, not because of righteous things we had done, but because of his mercy. He saved us through the washing of rebirth and renewal by the Holy Spirit, ⁶ whom he poured out on us generously through Jesus Christ our Savior, ⁷so that, having been justified by his grace, we might become heirs having the hope of eternal life. ⁸This is a trustworthy saying. And I want you to stress these things, so that those who have trusted in God may be careful to devote themselves to doing what is good. These things are excellent and profitable for everyone.

(c) What are your thoughts as a Servant leader concerning Scripture verses 1-8?

_____

_____

_____

_____

[9] But avoid foolish controversies and genealogies and arguments and quarrels about the law, because these are unprofitable and useless. [10] Warn a divisive person once, and then warn them a second time. After that, have nothing to do with them. [11] You may be sure that such people are warped and sinful; they are self-condemned."

(d) What are your thoughts as a Servant leader concerning Scripture verses 9-11?

_____

_____

_____

_____

_____

_____

_____

Activity #1B Obedience: Warnings and Benefits

(4) There are consequences in disobedience and benefits to obedience. Write out the following teachings from these Scripture verses:

Matthew 18:6 (Jesus speaks)

_____

_____

_____

_____

Colossians 2:4-5 (Paul)

_____

_____

_____

_____

Isaiah 9:16

_____

_____

_____

_____

Luke 21:8

_____

_____

_____

_____

Warning Against False Teachings And Deception

Avoiding Cult or Elitist

[1] "Then Jesus spoke to the multitudes and to His disciples, [2] saying: "The scribes and the Pharisees sit in Moses' seat. [3] Therefore whatever they tell you to observe, *that* observe and do, but do not do according to their works; for they say, and do not do. [4] For they bind heavy burdens, hard to bear, and lay *them* on men's shoulders; but they *themselves* will not move them with one of their fingers. [5] But all their works they do to be seen by men. They make their phylacteries (phy-lac-ter-y) broad and enlarge the borders of their garments. [6] They love the best places at feasts, the best seats in the synagogues, [7] greetings in the marketplaces, and to be called by men, 'Rabbi, Rabbi.' [8] But you, do not be called 'Rabbi'; for One is your Teacher, the Christ, and you are all brethren. [9] Do not call anyone on earth your father; for One is your Father, He who is in heaven. [10] And do not be called teachers; for One is your Teacher, the Christ. [11] But he who is greatest among you shall be your servant. [12] And whoever exalts himself will be humbled, and he who humbles himself will be exalted," Matthew 23:1-12 NKJV. "Take heed that no one deceives you. For many will come in My name, saying, 'I am the Christ,' and will deceive many," Matthew 24:4-5.

From literary and Biblical text, we find many examples of rulers who caused both physical and spiritual deaths of their followers. Even in today's modern times, there are religious sects identified as cults, defined by definition and function.

According to Merriam-Webster, the definition of cult is a system of religious beliefs regarded as unorthodox or false; having a body of members of great devotion to a person, idea, object, movement or work; consisting of leadership that functions as one of having an elitist attitude and biased beliefs in favor of a socially elite class of people.

In the days of Jeremiah and King Jehoiakim, there was a family among the Jewish community of Judah called the Rechabites Family. According to Judges 1:16, they were related to Moses by marriage and descendants of Rechab (Rekab) of the Midianites. This family was not considered, by people standards, to be worthy of any special place among the elitist of Israel. In fact, they were of sojourners who lived in tents within the community (Jeremiah 35). In the eyes of God, they were a people who obeyed the commands to worship Him and only Him (verse 16). They had fought King Ahab and were instrumental in removing the places of idol worship of Baal and restoring God's house of worship (2 Kings 10:15-31). In due season, for His purpose, God honored them before the people of Israel as obedient servant leaders.

> [18] And Jeremiah said to the house of the Rechabites, "Thus says the Lord of hosts, the God of Israel: 'Because you have obeyed the commandment of Jonadab your father, and kept all his precepts and done according to all

that he commanded you, [19] therefore thus says the Lord of hosts, the God of Israel: "Jonadab the son of Rechab shall not lack a man to stand before Me forever," Jeremiah 35:18-19.

The grace of God is unmeasurable and His judgment can be swift. God has promised to deal with leaders who mislead people; who promote untruths marred by falsehoods, meaningless platitudes, self-righteousness, self-gratification and insincere religious practices. He will punish groups and nations who refuse to be obedient and keep His word; who deals with cultist worship of false gods.

[17] "Therefore thus says the LORD: 'You have not obeyed Me in proclaiming liberty, everyone to his brother and everyone to his neighbor. Behold, I proclaim liberty to you,' says the LORD—'to the sword, to pestilence, and to famine! And I will deliver you to trouble among all the kingdoms of the earth. [18] And I will give the men who have transgressed My covenant, who have not performed the words of the covenant which they made before Me, when they cut the calf in two and passed between the parts of it— [19] the princes of Judah, the princes of Jerusalem, the eunuchs, the priests, and all the people of the land who passed between the parts of the calf— [20] I will give them into the hand of their enemies and into the hand of those who seek their life," Jeremiah 34:17-20.

As it was then, so is it today.

Servant leaders must be diligent to ask God for His divine covering; stand in the gap for family generations as leaders Jonadab and Job did for their families; pray with authority for protection against the evil of cult-like practices and leaders like Judah's King Zedekiah and the Jim Jones and Shoko Asahara.

As servant leaders, our service must meet the approval of God and not of man. This is the leadership that pleases God.

Activity #2 Required Service that Pleases God

God is concerned about the needs of people. Have faith in Him to know what is best for us.

Write out the following Scriptures about service that pleases God.

(a) James 2:14-17 _____

_____

_____

_____

(b) Luke 14:5; 13-14 _____

_____

_____

_____

(c) Romans 12:9-13 _____

_____

_____

_____

(d) Romans 12: 14-17;20 _____

_____

_____

_____

(e) I Peter 4:10 _____

_____

_____

_____

(f) 1 Peter 5:2-4 _____

_____

_____

_____

(g) Hebrews 10:24-25 _____

_____

_____

_____

_____

_____

Activity #3 Contend For the Faith

(1) Re-read the Book of Jude (Appendix).

How is following the advice of Jude in verses 20-23 a counterattack to false doctrine?

_____

_____

_____

_____

(2) In Matthew 23, Jesus calls attention to the leadership of the Scribes and Pharisees, as deceptive.

What will be the reward for those who lead in this matter? Refer to verses 13-14 in this Scripture.

_____

_____

_____

_____

(3) In this Scripture, 'contend' reflects that there is a challenge to maintain or deal with a situation. The word 'contend' is mentioned twice in this passage of Scripture.

How did Jude characterize these spots who were among the called people of God?

_____

_____

_____

What advice does he offer in verse 17?

_____

_____

_____

Activity #4 Required Forgiveness in Servant Leadership

Please God try to forgive those people
Because even if they say those bad things,
They don't know what they're doing.
So You could forgive them,
Just like You did those folks a long time ago
When they said terrible things about You.

-Ruby Bridges

This was the daily prayer of a little girl from the South, Ruby Bridges, as she faced a mob while she walked to school. Every morning those people taunted her because they did not want her to integrate their school. Although she was forced to comply to a court order, it made no difference to them. The hate was larger than their love. Her skin color was problematic to them. But for this kindergarten, God was greater than any hate and anyone - a lesson she learned from her Sunday School teacher and parents. She did not consider herself brave; she considered herself loved by God and God loved everyone.

Ruby led when she did not know she was leading. Ruby showed love and forgiveness when it was not shown to her. Leading by example is what our Lord Jesus did. She remembered that lesson. And when the time came, she demonstrated love in action to those who wanted no more than to take her life. She was God's servant! She was an example of a forgiving servant!

****

Unforgiveness Threatens Leadership and Creates Barriers!

Whether in the home, church or other environment, the servant cannot afford to not settle this account. Unfortunately, it is one of those areas that many Servant leaders elect to be indebted by.

In Matthew 18:21-35, Peter asked Jesus how often shall my brother sin against me and I forgive him? Apparently, Peter like the least of us, can hold on to unforgiveness and expect God's blessing in our actions.

An unforgiving heart will bring tragedy to the person who holds on to this disease: physical, mental, emotional and spiritual pain. Jesus does not want us to be bound by the tragedies of an unforgiving heart. The result could also mean generational curses and failure to walk in God's blessing! Jesus taught parables to help his followers understand the tragedy of an unforgiving heart and the rewards of a forgiving heart. Matthew 6:14-15

NKJV reads, "For if you forgive men their trespasses, your heavenly Father will also forgive you. [15] But if you do not forgive men their trespasses, neither will your Father forgive your trespasses."

> But a certain Samaritan, as he journeyed, came where he was. And when he saw him, he had compassion. So he went to *him* and bandaged his wounds, pouring on oil and wine; and he set him on his own animal, brought him to an inn, and took care of him. On the next day, when he departed, he took out two denarii, gave *them* to the innkeeper, and said to him, 'Take care of him; and whatever more you spend, when I come again, I will repay you.' So which of these three do you think was neighbor to him who fell among the thieves?" And he said, "He who showed mercy on him." Then Jesus said to him, "Go and do likewise," Luke 10:33-37.

It's Personal

In growing up, our family shared a great relationship with a very close family. The mother was so close to us, that we felt she was our "second" Mom and her siblings were our "brothers and sisters." Every day, we were a part of each other's lives. We were more than neighbors and friends; we were family. She taught us just as much about values and God as did our parents. This wonderful woman struggled to keep her family fed and clothed, but was always willing to share and help others. In fact, in one particular situation, she showed compassion toward a neighbor who had truly done her wrong. Years later when this neighbor became very sick, it was our beloved family friend who helped this ill lady neighbor. Her Christian actions are a reminder of Luke 10:33-37.

One day when my Mom, Ms. Mary and I were cleaning this sick neighbor's house, I witnessed the neighbor whom I will call Ms. Z, asking our friend Mom Mary for forgiveness. Ms. M, in her kindly voice, said, "I forgave you years ago; if I hadn't, I could not even be here right now taking care of you. God did this, not me. I was amazed at how Mom Mary handled this situation. I always thought she was a kindly Christian woman but her compassion is stamped into my *memory bank* as one of the most generous things I have ever witnessed.

Decades later, once again, I witnessed this type of forgiveness between my friend Rose and a school Administrator. As school leaders, we each had our individual styles in dealing with staff and each other. But this particular administrator was known for autocratic and unfriendly ways. She was especially demeaning and demanding toward my friend Rose, who was one of the most nurturing persons among us. In the workplace, Rose was known for her loving ways toward children and the staff. In fact, it was Rose, who taught me that what this person needed was really a friend and her bitterness was the result of fear. Lashing out, she said, was this administrator's leadership style; it was her way of protecting herself.

Somewhere in her life, Rose reemphasized, that perhaps this woman had experienced a terrible hurt. Needless to say, I found no comfort in Rose's words - at least, at first. But I agreed to meet with Rose each morning prior to work, and secretly pray for specific changes that will yield the good fruit that pleases God. This went on for years. And one day, I witnessed a great surprise. I witnessed this Administrator asked my friend, Rose, for forgiveness about the way she had treated her over the years. Rose responded to her, "It's alright. I know this is really not who you want to be. I pray for you every day and I will continue to pray for you." Two weeks after that experience, Rose, unexpectedly, had heart failure and passed. The Administrator and I never talked about the time she asked for that forgiveness from Rose; we did not have a "friendly" relationship – only a work relationship. But one day, unexpectedly, the administrator had a problem in the Media Center. She looked at me and said, "Rose would have seen this coming." I responded, "She would have handled the situation before it got to you." I took her statement as a sign of respect and that she missed Rose as I did; and perhaps was glad that she had been forgiven for mistreating this woman of God.

Forgiveness versus Unforgiveness

In the flesh, yes, most persons want to settle accounts by returning an eye-for-an eye. As your relationship deepens with God, the spirit-man learns how to "man' the battlefield with spiritual weapons. The reactions of Ruby Bridges and King David were not that of eye-for-an-eye as they faced their enemies. In fact, their responses made them stronger than their enemies.

(1) How is Ruby Bridges' actions in dealing with a mob similar to David's actions in dealing with Saul? Refer back to the Scriptures.

_____

_____

_____

_____

(2) Unforgiveness gives the person power over you. Asking God for that release from unforgiveness will bring health in mind, body and spirit. Psalm 51:10 NKJV says, "Create in me a clean heart, O God, And renew a steadfast spirit within me."

There are several Scriptures in the Word of God about forgiveness. For example, Matthew 6:14-15, "For if you forgive other people when they sin against you, your heavenly Father will also forgive you. But if you do not forgive others their sins, your Father will not forgive your sins." Forgiveness is a central attribute in following the example of Christ." The Scriptures listed below are only a few examples.

Isaiah 43:25 - I, *even* I, *am* He who blots out your transgressions for My own sake; And I will not remember your sins.

Micah 7:18-19 - Who *is* a God like You, Pardoning iniquity And passing over the transgression of the remnant of His heritage? He does not retain His anger forever, Because He delights *in* mercy. He will again have compassion on us, And will subdue our iniquities. You will cast all our sins Into the depths of the sea.

Mark 11: 25 - And whenever you stand praying, if you have anything against anyone, forgive him, that your Father in heaven may also forgive you your trespasses.

Colossians 1:12-14 - giving thanks to the Father who has qualified us to be partakers of the inheritance of the saints in the light. He has delivered us from the power of darkness and conveyed *us* into the kingdom of the Son of His love, in whom we have redemption through His blood, the forgiveness of sins.

Locate and write out the following Scriptures about forgiveness:

Matthew 6:12

_____

_____

_____

Matthew 5:43-45

_____

_____

_____

Luke 23:34

_____

_____

_____

Luke 17:3-4

_____

_____

_____

Ephesians 4:32

_____

_____

_____

(3) What are your thoughts concerning forgiveness?

_____

_____

_____

Activity #5 Be-in-Attitude

Matthew 5 NKJV The Beatitudes

And seeing the multitudes, He went up on a mountain, and when He was seated His disciples came to Him.

Then He opened His mouth and taught them, saying:

Blessed *are* the poor in spirit, For theirs is the kingdom of heaven.

Blessed *are* those who mourn, For they shall be comforted.

Blessed *are* the meek, For they shall inherit the earth.

Blessed *are* those who hunger and thirst for righteousness, For they shall be filled.

Blessed *are* the merciful, For they shall obtain mercy.

Blessed *are* the pure in heart, For they shall see God.

Blessed *are* the peacemakers, For they shall be called sons of God.

Blessed *are* those who are persecuted for righteousness' sake, For theirs is the kingdom of heaven. Blessed are you when they revile and persecute you, and say all kinds of evil against you falsely for My sake.

Rejoice and be exceedingly glad, for great *is* your reward in heaven, for so they persecuted the prophets who were before you.

(1) Based on The Beatitudes, what trait do you "see" operating in Ms. Mary toward a sick neighbor?

_____

_____

_____

(2) Based on The Beatitudes, what trait do you "see" at work in Rose?

_____

_____

_____

(3) If attitude determines altitude, based on Matthew 5, what has kept you from "going higher?"

_____

_____

_____

Activity #6 Father Forgive Them

In Matthew 5, words such as mercy, peacemakers, pure in hear, and rejoice are mentioned as blessings that generates rewards. James 2:13 amplifies that mercy triumphs over judgment. Jesus demonstrated this type of mercy toward his enemies and every day God gives us new mercy. At the cross, Jesus taking on our sins, did so for our salvation. His prayer of forgiveness was: "Father, forgive them, for they do not know what they do." *Luke 24:34 NKJV.*

Stephen, an apostle of Christ cried out to The Lord to forgive his enemies: "And they stoned Stephen as he was calling on *God* and saying, "Lord Jesus, receive my spirit." [60] Then he knelt down and cried out with a loud voice, "Lord, do not charge them with this sin." And when he had said this, he fell asleep." *Acts 7:59-60 NKJV.*

In following Christ, then the expectation of leaders, is to forgive. As servant leaders, we are accountable to God. Both forgiveness and unforgiveness is connected to the effectiveness of your ministry as a Servant leader. Let's look closer at Scriptures that stresses forgiveness, mercy, peace, as serving God.

(1) Write out Scripture Matthew 18:21-22.

_____

_____

_____

_____

(2) Write out the line from the Lord's Prayer Luke11 concerning forgiveness.

_____

_____

_____

_____

(3) Write out Matthew 6: 14-15.

_____

_____

_____

_____

(4) Read Romans 12:9-21 concerning Christian behavior. What should be your attitude toward others in service to God?

_____

_____

_____

_____

_____

_____

(5) Write out Romans 12:1-2.

_____

_____

_____

_____

_____

_____

(6) Let's be honest. It takes the love of God to show us how to forgive and serve. Ruby Bridges learned this from her Sunday School teachers. How can you teach this principle to a child?

_____

_____

_____

SECTION IV: RESPONSBILE SERVANT-LEADERSHIP TAKEAWAYS

What are some Key Takeaways that stood out for you? Takeaways might include anything that resonates with you. It might include experiences, challenges, loves, emotions, or changes.

Key Takeaways

You may not have key takeaways in each area.

Experience(s):

Challenge(s):

Love(s)

Emotion(s)

Change (s)

Other:

SECTION V: UNLIKELY SERVANT LEADERS

In this section, you will have the opportunity to reflect upon your personal calling to Servant leadership.

CONTENT LESSONS AND ACTIVITIES

Unlikely Servant Leaders
- ❖ Activity #1 – Reflect Upon Psalm 91
- ❖ Activity #2 - Personal Prayer

A Citizenry Change
- ❖ Activity #3 – Self Description – What is your resume?
- ❖ Activity #4 – My Personal Plan of Action

Personal Takeaway – Your Plan of Action

Unlikely Servant Leaders

In ancient and modern times, God has purposely chosen people from the beginning of man's creation to carry out His assignments. In Biblical times, these figures came from different backgrounds and occupations; i.e., The Twelve Disciples, Rahab, Jonah, Esther, David, the Wailing Women, Israel's Judges, Jeremiah, Aaron, Paul, Mary the Mother of Jesus, John the Baptist, and appointed musicians. Jesus, both divine and human, struggled with his assignment as the time drew near for him to take on the sins of this world. Yet, he knew his purpose was God's Will. We recall the stories of ordinary people who struggled with their calling, and found their strength in obeying God, i.e., Jonah and Paul:

➤ **Paul** – "And I, brethren, when I came to you, did not come with excellence of speech or of wisdom declaring to you the testimony of God. [2] For I determined not to know anything among you except Jesus Christ and Him crucified. [3] I was with you in weakness, in fear, and in much trembling. [4] And my speech and my preaching *were* not with persuasive words of human wisdom, but in demonstration of the Spirit and of power, [5] that your faith should not be in the wisdom of men but in the power of God," 1 Corinthians 2:1-5 NKJV.

➤ **Nehemiah** – "O Lord, I pray, please let Your ear be attentive to the prayer of Your servant, and to the prayer of Your servants who desire to fear Your name; and let Your servant prosper this day, I pray, and grant him mercy in the sight of this man," Nehemiah 1:11 NKJV.

➤ **Esther** – "Then Esther told *them* to reply to Mordecai: [16] "Go, gather all the Jews who are present in Shushan, and fast for me; neither eat nor drink for three days, night or day. My maids and I will fast likewise. And so I will go to the king, which *is* against the law; and if I perish, I perish!" Esther 4:15-16 NKJV.

➤ **David** – "Have mercy upon me, O God, According to Your lovingkindness; According to the multitude of Your tender mercies, Blot out my transgressions. Wash me thoroughly from my iniquity, And cleanse me from my sin," Psalm 51:2 NKJV.

➤ **Rahab** – "Now therefore, I beg you, swear to me by the Lord, since I have shown you kindness, that you also will show kindness to my father's house, and give me a true token, and spare my father, my mother, my brothers, my sisters, and all that they have, and deliver our lives from death," Joshua 2:13 NKJV.

➤ **Jonah** – "Then Jonah prayed to the Lord his God from the fish's belly. And he said: "I cried out to the Lord because of my affliction, And He answered me," Jonah 2:2 NKJV.

➤ **Stephen** - When they heard these things they were cut to the heart, and they gnashed at him with *their* teeth. [55] But he, being full of the Holy Spirit, gazed into heaven and saw the glory of God, and Jesus standing at the right hand of God, [56] and said, "Look! I see the heavens opened and the Son of Man standing at the right hand of God!" Acts 7:54 NKJV

With God's aid, these men and women went forth in their assignments. While each was unique, all were in need of God in fulfilling their assignments.

"Our help *is* in the name of the Lord, Who made heaven and earth," Psalm 124:8 NKJV.

Activity #1 Psalm 91

(1) Read the following: Psalm 91 NKJV

He who dwells in the secret place of the Most High
Shall abide under the shadow of the Almighty.
[2] I will say of the LORD, "*He is* my refuge and my fortress;
My God, in Him I will trust."
[3] Surely He shall deliver you from the snare of the fowler
And from the perilous pestilence.
[4] He shall cover you with His feathers,
And under His wings you shall take refuge;
His truth *shall be your* shield and buckler.
[5] You shall not be afraid of the terror by night,
Nor of the arrow *that* flies by day,
[6] *Nor* of the pestilence *that* walks in darkness,
Nor of the destruction *that* lays waste at noonday.

[7] A thousand may fall at your side, And ten thousand at your right hand;
But it shall not come near you.
[8] Only with your eyes shall you look, And see the reward of the wicked.

[9] Because you have made the LORD, *who is* my refuge, *Even* the Most High, your dwelling place,
[10] No evil shall befall you, Nor shall any plague come near your dwelling;
[11] For He shall give His angels charge over you, To keep you in all your ways.
[12] In *their* hands they shall bear you up, Lest you dash your foot against a stone.
[13] You shall tread upon the lion and the cobra,
The young lion and the serpent you shall trample underfoot.

[14] "Because he has set his love upon Me, therefore I will deliver him; I will set him on high, because he has known My name.
[15] He shall call upon Me, and I will answer him;
I *will be* with him in trouble; I will deliver him and honor him.
[16] With long life I will satisfy him, And show him My salvation."

(2) Do you feel a praise – a praise to God for his covering, a dwelling place in Him (Psalm 91)? Give God thanksgiving for such a glorious promise. Just as he chose so many others, He has chosen you as an 'unlikely leader."

Activity #2 Your Personal Prayer

A Citizenry Change

It is most unlikely that you see yourself as a national leader (by man's standards). But when one accepts Christ in their life, one becomes part of the body of Christ. **Your citizenry has changed.** You are physically located in this world but not of this world. As part of the body of Christ, you have received special orders as part of this citizenry: it is an appointment; it is a commission to evangelize and lead others to Christ. By God's standards, we are Kingdom Leaders. Yes, our past makes us unlikely leaders but because of His grace and mercy, we have been called to serve.

God knows all about our weaknesses; but He has chosen to use us. So, lean not on your own understanding - lean on Him. Trust Him that you will become the leader He has created you to be for such a time as this. This is not an unfamiliar road to God, only to us. You will be identifiable as a servant leader, however unlikely, if you follow His Will and not yours.

Unlikely leaders are identifiable by how they treat others.

In earlier sections of this book, we highlighted some unlikely world and Biblical leaders. Let's take a closer look at one modern-time leader who has a resume of an unlikely leader – Oprah, whose name was taken from the Bible (although misspelled).

As a young child, her resume read:

- Born in poverty in rural Kosciusko, Mississippi in 1954
- Named after the biblical figure in the Book of Ruth (Orpah)
- Born out of wedlock to a teen-age mother and young father
- Learned to read by age 3
- Raised by a God-fearing, abusive grandmother until the age of 6
- Relocated to Milwaukee, Wisconsin to live in a single-parent home
- Raped by a cousin at the age of 9
- Continued physical and sexual abuse by other male relatives and Mother's boyfriend
- Ran away from home at the age of 13
- Became pregnant at the age of 14; child died after giving birth
- Sent to live with strict father and stepmom in Nashville, Tennessee

This does not seem to be the resume of a billionaire woman – a media mogul, a giant of a leader in the business world today. But this the beginnings of media mogul OPRAH WINFREY.

Oprah, as a journalist, being truthful to herself, has spoken often about her childhood, abusive situations, and of those who helped her along the way. She learned about the Bible from her grandmother; from her she learned how to read and write before the age of three. It was in the church that she was given the name "The Little Speaker." She was given the opportunity to recite poems and participate in speaking contests in the church.

She credits the decision that her mother (Venita Lee) made to send a troubled child (Oprah) to live with her father (Vernon Winfrey and her stepmother. It was in this home that her education flourished; under the discipline of her father, life changed:

- 1971 First African American to be named Miss Nashville Fire Prevention
- 1971 Graduated with honors from East Memphis High School
- 1971 Placed second in the nation for dramatic interpretation
- 1971 Received full scholarship to Tennessee State University
- 1973 Became the youngest (age 19) and first female anchor for WTVF-TV, Nashville.

Today, Oprah is a media mogul, actress, producer and philanthropist who credits God for her journey and who has helped her to stand – she believes in waiting for His marching orders.

> **"I have church with myself: I have church walking down the street. I believe in the God force that lives inside all of us, and once you tap into that, you can do anything.**
>
> "Doubt means don't. When you don't know what to do, do nothing until you do know what to do. Because the doubt is your inner voice or the voice of God or whatever you choose to call it. It is your instinct trying to tell you something is off. That's how I have found myself to be led spiritually, because that's your spiritual voice saying to you, 'let's think about it.' So when you don't know what to do, do nothing."

Her "firsts" are many. For example, in 1990, became the first African American woman to be named one of the most influential people in entertainment by Entertainment Weekly. Today, she is ranked among the "50 most generous Americans."

Unlikely leaders are tested and refined for His glory. Isaiah 48:10 NIV, "I have refined you, though not as silver; I have tested you in the furnace of affliction." Your desire is to serve. There is a difference between leadership and Servant leadership. Servant leadership is of God. *No prerequisites to His election are from man; God's choosing or elected is as believers.* Romans 8:29 states "Whom he foreknew he also foreordained to be conformed to the image of his Son." So, why does it take us by surprise when we are given the opportunity to be serve? Perhaps because we know that we are unworthy of this honor; and out of fear of the unknown we want to step back rather than go forth. But God has an answer for this. "Lean not on your own understanding, lean on the Creator."

Unlikely servant leaders are grateful. They know what it is to give thanks to be counted among those who are called to serve in His kingdom. You marvel at the amazement of the Father, the work of Jesus the Christ, and the gift of the Holy Spirit. It makes you so grateful that the Father took the time to nurture you in His Kingdom. 2 Thess. 2:13 states, "But we are bound to give thanks to God always for you, brethren, beloved of the Lord, for that God chose you from the beginning unto salvation in sanctification of the Spirit and belief of the truth."

Yes, unlikely leaders, you have been chosen from the beginning, but it is in respect of God's actions and not by your own merits.

Activity #3 Self-Description: What is Your Resume?

In this activity, you will reflect upon YOUR resume as an unlikely leader. Begin to write a self-description starting with your early years.

<u>My Childhood</u>

As a child

Early Education

Special Memories

Likes

Dislikes

If I could change something about my childhood, it would be

My religious background as a child

Whom Am I Now

I describe myself as

I desire

My hopes

My challenges

My strengths

My gifts

Activity #4 Your Personal Plan of Action

Based on your personal assessment and prayers, what plan of action will you take to ensure you are on God agenda?

Actions	Based on Personal Assessment	Based on Personal Prayer

Notes: _____

_____

_____

_____

APPENDIX - SCRIPTURES

Ephesians 6:

14-20 NKJV

14 Stand therefore, having girded your waist with truth, having put on the breastplate of righteousness, 15 and having shod your feet with the preparation of the gospel of peace; 16 above all, taking the shield of faith with which you will be able to quench all the fiery darts of the wicked one. 17 And take the helmet of salvation, and the sword of the Spirit, which is the word of God; 18 praying always with all prayer and supplication in the Spirit, being watchful to this end with all perseverance and supplication for all the saints— 19 and for me, that utterance may be given to me, that I may open my mouth boldly to make known the mystery of the gospel, 20 for which I am an ambassador in chains; that in it I may speak boldly, as I ought to speak.

Exodus 18: 17-21 NKJV

17 So Moses' father-in-law said to him, "The thing that you do is not good. 18 Both you and these people who are with you will surely wear yourselves out. For this thing is too much for you; you are not able to perform it by yourself. 19 Listen now to my voice; I will give you counsel, and God will be with you: Stand before God for the people, so that you may bring the difficulties to God. 20 And you shall teach them the statutes and the laws, and show them the way in which they must walk and the work they must do. 21 Moreover you shall select from all the people able men, such as fear God, men of truth, hating covetousness; and place such over them to be rulers of thousands, rulers of hundreds, rulers of fifties, and rulers of tens.

Ezekiel 1:1-22 NKJV

Ezekiel's Vision of God

1 Now it came to pass in the thirtieth year, in the fourth *month,* on the fifth *day* of the month, as I *was* among the captives by the River Chebar, *that* the heavens were opened and I saw visions of God. 2 On the fifth *day* of the month, which *was* in the fifth year of King Jehoiachin's captivity, 3 the word of the LORD came expressly to Ezekiel the priest, the son of Buzi, in the land of the Chaldeans by the River Chebar; and the hand of the LORD was upon him there.

4 Then I looked, and behold, a whirlwind was coming out of the north, a great cloud with raging fire engulfing itself; and brightness *was* all around it and radiating out of its midst like the color of amber, out of the midst of the fire. 5 Also from within it *came* the likeness of four living creatures. And this *was* their appearance: they had the likeness of a man. 6

Each one had four faces, and each one had four wings. 7 Their legs *were* straight, and the soles of their feet *were* like the soles of calves' feet. They sparkled like the color of burnished bronze. 8 The hands of a man *were* under their wings on their four sides; and each of the four had faces and wings. 9 Their wings touched one another. *The creatures* did not turn when they went, but each one went straight forward.

10 As for the likeness of their faces, *each* had the face of a man; each of the four had the face of a lion on the right side, each of the four had the face of an ox on the left side, and each of the four had the face of an eagle. 11 Thus *were* their faces. Their wings stretched upward; two *wings* of each one touched one another, and two covered their bodies. 12 And each one went straight forward; they went wherever the spirit wanted to go, and they did not turn when they went.

13 As for the likeness of the living creatures, their appearance *was* like burning coals of fire, like the appearance of torches going back and forth among the living creatures. The fire was bright, and out of the fire went lightning. 14 And the living creatures ran back and forth, in appearance like a flash of lightning.

15 Now as I looked at the living creatures, behold, a wheel *was* on the earth beside each living creature with its four faces. 16 The appearance of the wheels and their workings *was* like the color of beryl, and all four had the same likeness. The appearance of their workings *was,* as it were, a wheel in the middle of a wheel. 17 When they moved, they went toward any one of four directions; they did not turn aside when they went. 18 As for their rims, they were so high they were awesome; and their rims *were* full of eyes, all around the four of them. 19 When the living creatures went, the wheels went beside them; and when the living creatures were lifted up from the earth, the wheels were lifted up. 20 Wherever the spirit wanted to go, they went, *because* there the spirit went; and the wheels were lifted together with them, for the spirit of the living creatures *was* in the wheels. 21 When those went, *these* went; when those stood, *these* stood; and when those were lifted up from the earth, the wheels were lifted up together with them, for the spirit of the living creatures *was* in the wheels.

22 The likeness of the firmament above the heads of the living creatures *was* like the color of an awesome crystal, stretched out over their heads.

Ezekiel 4:1-8 NKJV

The Siege of Jerusalem Portrayed

1 "You also, son of man, take a clay tablet and lay it before you, and portray on it a city, Jerusalem. 2 Lay siege against it, build a siege wall against it, and heap up a mound against it; set camps against it also, and place battering rams against it all around. 3 Moreover take

for yourself an iron plate, and set it *as* an iron wall between you and the city. Set your face against it, and it shall be besieged, and you shall lay siege against it. This *will be* a sign to the house of Israel. 4 "Lie also on your left side, and lay the iniquity of the house of Israel upon it. *According* to the number of the days that you lie on it, you shall bear their iniquity. 5 For I have laid on you the years of their iniquity, according to the number of the days, three hundred and ninety days; so you shall bear the iniquity of the house of Israel. 6 And when you have completed them, lie again on your right side; then you shall bear the iniquity of the house of Judah forty days. I have laid on you a day for each year. 7 "Therefore you shall set your face toward the siege of Jerusalem; your arm *shall be* uncovered, and you shall prophesy against it. 8 And surely I will restrain you so that you cannot turn from one side to another till you have ended the days of your siege.

Ezekiel 33:1-9 NKJV

Again the word of the Lord came to me, saying, 2 "Son of man, speak to the children of your people, and say to them: 'When I bring the sword upon a land, and the people of the land take a man from their territory and make him their watchman, 3 when he sees the sword coming upon the land, if he blows the trumpet and warns the people, 4 then whoever hears the sound of the trumpet and does not take warning, if the sword comes and takes him away, his blood shall be on his *own* head. 5 He heard the sound of the trumpet, but did not take warning; his blood shall be upon himself. But he who takes warning will [a]save his life. 6 But if the watchman sees the sword coming and does not blow the trumpet, and the people are not warned, and the sword comes and takes *any* person from among them, he is taken away in his iniquity; but his blood I will require at the watchman's hand.' 7 "So you, son of man: I have made you a watchman for the house of Israel; therefore you shall hear a word from My mouth and warn them for Me. 8 When I say to the wicked, 'O wicked *man,* you shall surely die!' and you do not speak to warn the wicked from his way, that wicked *man* shall die in his iniquity; but his blood I will require at your hand. 9 Nevertheless if you warn the wicked to turn from his way, and he does not turn from his way, he shall die in his iniquity; but you have delivered your soul.

3 John Chapter 1:1-14 NKJV

Greeting to Gaius

1 The Elder,

To the beloved Gaius, whom I love in truth:

2 Beloved, I pray that you may prosper in all things and be in health, just as your soul prospers. 3 For I rejoiced greatly when brethren came and testified of the truth *that is* in

you, just as you walk in the truth. 4 I have no greater joy than to hear that my children walk in truth.

Gaius Commended for Generosity

5 Beloved, you do faithfully whatever you do for the brethren and for strangers, 6 who have borne witness of your love before the church. *If* you send them forward on their journey in a manner worthy of God, you will do well, 7 because they went forth for His name's sake, taking nothing from the Gentiles.

8 We therefore ought to receive such, that we may become fellow workers for the truth.

Diotrephes and Demetrius

9 I wrote to the church, but Diotrephes, who loves to have the preeminence among them, does not receive us. 10 Therefore, if I come, I will call to mind his deeds which he does, prating against us with malicious words. And not content with that, he himself does not receive the brethren, and forbids those who wish to, putting *them* out of the church.

11 Beloved, do not imitate what is evil, but what is good. He who does good is of God, but he who does evil has not seen God.

12 Demetrius has a *good* testimony from all, and from the truth itself. And we also bear witness, and you know that our testimony is true.

Farewell Greeting

13 I had many things to write, but I do not wish to write to you with pen and ink; 14 but I hope to see you shortly, and we shall speak face to face.

Peace to you. Our friends greet you. Greet the friends by name.

Jude

Greeting to the Called

1 Jude, a bondservant of Jesus Christ, and brother of James,
To those who are called, sanctified by God the Father, and preserved in Jesus Christ:
2 Mercy, peace, and love be multiplied to you.

Contend for the Faith

3 Beloved, while I was very diligent to write to you concerning our common salvation, I found it necessary to write to you exhorting you to contend earnestly for the faith which was once for all delivered to the saints. 4 For certain men have crept in unnoticed, who long ago were marked out for this condemnation, ungodly men, who turn the grace of our God into lewdness and deny the only Lord God and our Lord Jesus Christ.

Old and New Apostates [a]

5 But I want to remind you, though you once knew this, that the Lord, having saved the people out of the land of Egypt, afterward destroyed those who did not believe.

6 And the angels who did not keep their proper domain, but left their own abode, He has reserved in everlasting chains under darkness for the judgment of the great day;

7 as Sodom and Gomorrah, and the cities around them in a similar manner to these, having given themselves over to sexual immorality and gone after strange flesh, are set forth as an example, suffering the vengeance of eternal fire.

8 Likewise also these dreamers defile the flesh, reject authority, and speak evil of dignitaries.

9 Yet Michael the archangel, in contending with the devil, when he disputed about the body of Moses, dared not bring against him a reviling accusation, but said, "The Lord rebuke you!"

10 But these speak evil of whatever they do not know; and whatever they know naturally, like brute beasts, in these things they corrupt themselves.

11 Woe to them! For they have gone in the way of Cain, have run greedily in the error of Balaam for profit, and perished in the rebellion of Korah.

Apostates Depraved and Doomed

12 These are spots in your love feasts, while they feast with you without fear, serving *only* themselves. *They are* clouds without water, carried about by the winds; late autumn trees without fruit, twice dead, pulled up by the roots; 13 raging waves of the sea, foaming up their own shame; wandering stars for whom is reserved the blackness of darkness forever.

14 Now Enoch, the seventh from Adam, prophesied about these men also, saying, "Behold, the Lord comes with ten thousands of His saints,

15 to execute judgment on all, to convict all who are ungodly among them of all their ungodly deeds which they have committed in an ungodly way, and of all the harsh things which ungodly sinners have spoken against Him."

Apostates Predicted

16 These are grumblers, complainers, walking according to their own lusts; and they mouth great swelling *words*, flattering people to gain advantage. 17 But you, beloved, remember the words which were spoken before by the apostles of our Lord Jesus Christ:

18 how they told you that there would be mockers in the last time who would walk according to their own ungodly lusts. 19 These are sensual persons, who cause divisions, not having the Spirit.

Maintain Your Life with God

20 But you, beloved, building yourselves up on your most holy faith, praying in the Holy Spirit,

21 keep yourselves in the love of God, looking for the mercy of our Lord Jesus Christ unto eternal life.

22 And on some have compassion, making a distinction;

23 but others save with fear, pulling them out of the fire, hating even the garment defiled by the flesh.

Glory to God

24 Now to Him who is able to keep you from stumbling, And to present you faultless Before the presence of His glory with exceeding joy,

25 To God our Savior, Who alone is wise, Be glory and majesty, Dominion and power, Both now and forever. Amen.

[a] person who renounces a religious or political belief or principle.

Judges 4:1-10 NKJV

1 When Ehud was dead, the children of Israel again did evil in the sight of the LORD. 2 So the LORD sold them into the hand of Jabin king of Canaan, who reigned in Hazor. The commander of his army *was* Sisera, who dwelt in Harosheth Hagoyim. 3 And the children of Israel cried out to the LORD; for Jabin had nine hundred chariots of iron, and for twenty years he had harshly oppressed the children of Israel.

4 Now Deborah, a prophetess, the wife of Lapidoth, was judging Israel at that time. 5 And she would sit under the palm tree of Deborah between Ramah and Bethel in the mountains of Ephraim. And the children of Israel came up to her for judgment. 6 Then she sent and called for Barak the son of Abinoam from Kedesh in Naphtali, and said to him, "Has not the LORD God of Israel commanded, 'Go and deploy *troops* at Mount Tabor; take with you ten thousand men of the sons of Naphtali and of the sons of Zebulun; 7 and against you I will deploy Sisera, the commander of Jabin's army, with his chariots and his multitude at the River Kishon; and I will deliver him into your hand'?"

8 And Barak said to her, "If you will go with me, then I will go; but if you will not go with me, I will not go!"

9 So she said, "I will surely go with you; nevertheless there will be no glory for you in the journey you are taking, for the LORD will sell Sisera into the hand of a woman." Then Deborah arose and went with Barak to Kedesh. 10 And Barak called Zebulun and Naphtali to Kedesh; he went up with ten thousand men under his command, and Deborah went up with him.

1 Samuel 17: 32-50 NKJV

32 Then David said to Saul, "Let no man's heart fail because of him; your servant will go and fight with this Philistine."

33 And Saul said to David, "You are not able to go against this Philistine to fight with him; for you *are* a youth, and he a man of war from his youth."

34 But David said to Saul, "Your servant used to keep his father's sheep, and when a lion or a bear came and took a lamb out of the flock, 35 I went out after it and struck it, and delivered *the lamb* from its mouth; and when it arose against me, I caught *it* by its beard, and struck and killed it. 36 Your servant has killed both lion and bear; and this uncircumcised Philistine will be like one of them, seeing he has defied the armies of the living God." 37 Moreover David said, "The Lord, who delivered me from the paw of the lion and from the paw of the bear, He will deliver me from the hand of this Philistine."

And Saul said to David, "Go, and the Lord be with you!"

38 So Saul clothed David with his armor, and he put a bronze helmet on his head; he also clothed him with a coat of mail. 39 David fastened his sword to his armor and tried to walk, for he had not tested *them*. And David said to Saul, "I cannot walk with these, for I have not tested *them*." So David took them off.

40 Then he took his staff in his hand; and he chose for himself five smooth stones from the brook, and put them in a shepherd's bag, in a pouch which he had, and his sling was in his hand. And he drew near to the Philistine. 41 So the Philistine came, and began drawing near to David, and the man who bore the shield *went* before him. 42 And when the Philistine looked about and saw David, he disdained him; for he was *only* a youth, ruddy and good-looking. 43 So the Philistine said to David, "*Am* I a dog, that you come to me with sticks?" And the Philistine cursed David by his gods. 44 And the Philistine said to David, "Come to me, and I will give your flesh to the birds of the air and the beasts of the field!"

45 Then David said to the Philistine, "You come to me with a sword, with a spear, and with a javelin. But I come to you in the name of the Lord of hosts, the God of the armies of Israel, whom you have defied. 46 This day the Lord will deliver you into my hand, and I will strike you and take your head from you. And this day I will give the carcasses of the camp of the Philistines to the birds of the air and the wild beasts of the earth, that all the earth may know that there is a God in Israel. 47 Then all this assembly shall know that the Lord does not save with sword and spear; for the battle *is* the Lord's, and He will give you into our hands."

48 So it was, when the Philistine arose and came and drew near to meet David, that David hurried and ran toward the army to meet the Philistine. 49 Then David put his hand in his bag and took out a stone; and he slung *it* and struck the Philistine in his forehead, so that the stone sank into his forehead, and he fell on his face to the earth. 50 So David prevailed over the Philistine with a sling and a stone, and struck the Philistine and killed him. But *there was* no sword in the hand of David.

1 Samuel 18:1-29 NKJV

Now when he had finished speaking to Saul, the soul of Jonathan was knit to the soul of David, and Jonathan loved him as his own soul. 2 Saul took him that day, and would not let him go home to his father's house anymore. 3 Then Jonathan and David made a covenant, because he loved him as his own soul. 4 And Jonathan took off the robe that was on him and gave it to David, with his armor, even to his sword and his bow and his belt.

5 So David went out wherever Saul sent him, and behaved wisely. And Saul set him over the men of war, and he was accepted in the sight of all the people and also in the sight

of Saul's servants. 6 Now it had happened as they were coming home, when David was returning from the slaughter of the Philistine, that the women had come out of all the cities of Israel, singing and dancing, to meet King Saul, with tambourines, with joy, and with musical instruments. 7 So the women sang as they danced, and said:

"Saul has slain his thousands, And David his ten thousands."

8 Then Saul was very angry, and the saying displeased him; and he said, "They have ascribed to David ten thousands, and to me they have ascribed only thousands. Now what more can he have but the kingdom?" 9 So Saul eyed David from that day forward.

10 And it happened on the next day that the distressing spirit from God came upon Saul, and he prophesied inside the house. So David played music with his hand, as at other times; but there was a spear in Saul's hand. 11 And Saul cast the spear, for he said, "I will pin David to the wall!" But David escaped his presence twice.

12 Now Saul was afraid of David, because the Lord was with him, but had departed from Saul. 13 Therefore Saul removed him from his presence, and made him his captain over a thousand; and he went out and came in before the people. 14 And David behaved wisely in all his ways, and the Lord was with him. 15 Therefore, when Saul saw that he behaved very wisely, he was afraid of him. 16 But all Israel and Judah loved David, because he went out and came in before them.

David Marries Michal

17 Then Saul said to David, "Here is my older daughter Merab; I will give her to you as a wife. Only be valiant for me, and fight the Lord's battles." For Saul thought, "Let my hand not be against him, but let the hand of the Philistines be against him."

18 So David said to Saul, "Who am I, and what is my life or my father's family in Israel, that I should be son-in-law to the king?" 19 But it happened at the time when Merab, Saul's daughter, should have been given to David, that she was given to Adriel the Meholathite as a wife.

20 Now Michal, Saul's daughter, loved David. And they told Saul, and the thing pleased him. 21 So Saul said, "I will give her to him, that she may be a snare to him, and that the hand of the Philistines may be against him." Therefore Saul said to David a second time, "You shall be my son-in-law today."

22 And Saul commanded his servants, "Communicate with David secretly, and say, 'Look, the king has delight in you, and all his servants love you. Now therefore, become the king's son-in-law.'

23 So Saul's servants spoke those words in the hearing of David. And David said, "Does it seem to you a light thing to be a king's son-in-law, seeing I am a poor and lightly esteemed man?" 24 And the servants of Saul told him, saying, In this manner David spoke."

25 Then Saul said, "Thus you shall say to David: 'The king does not desire any dowry but one hundred foreskins of the Philistines, to take vengeance on the king's enemies.' " But Saul thought to make David fall by the hand of the Philistines. 26 So when his servants told David these words, it pleased David well to become the king's son-in-law. Now the days had not expired; 27 therefore David arose and went, he and his men, and killed two hundred men of the Philistines. And David brought their foreskins, and they gave them in full count to the king, that he might become the king's son-in-law. Then Saul gave him Michal his daughter as a wife.

28 Thus Saul saw and knew that the Lord was with David, and that Michal, Saul's daughter, loved him; 29 and Saul was still more afraid of David. So Saul became David's enemy continually. 30 Then the princes of the Philistines went out to war. And so it was, whenever they went out, that David behaved more wisely than all the servants of Saul, so that his name became highly esteemed.

1 Samuel 19:1-24 NKJV

Now Saul spoke to Jonathan his son and to all his servants, that they should kill David; but Jonathan, Saul's son, delighted greatly in David. 2 So Jonathan told David, saying, "My father Saul seeks to kill you. Therefore please be on your guard until morning, and stay in a secret place and hide. 3 And I will go out and stand beside my father in the field where you are, and I will speak with my father about you. Then what I observe, I will tell you."

4 Thus Jonathan spoke well of David to Saul his father, and said to him, "Let not the king sin against his servant, against David, because he has not sinned against you, and because his works have been very good toward you. 5 For he took his life in his hands and killed the Philistine, and the Lord brought about a great deliverance for all Israel. You saw it and rejoiced. Why then will you sin against innocent blood, to kill David without a cause?"

6 So Saul heeded the voice of Jonathan, and Saul swore, "As the Lord lives, he shall not be killed." 7 Then Jonathan called David, and Jonathan told him all these things. So Jonathan brought David to Saul, and he was in his presence as in times past.

8 And there was war again; and David went out and fought with the Philistines, and struck them with a mighty blow, and they fled from him.

9 Now the distressing spirit from the Lord came upon Saul as he sat in his house with his spear in his hand. And David was playing music with his hand. 10 Then Saul sought to pin

David to the wall with the spear, but he slipped away from Saul's presence; and he drove the spear into the wall. So David fled and escaped that night.

11 Saul also sent messengers to David's house to watch him and to kill him in the morning. And Michal, David's wife, told him, saying, "If you do not save your life tonight, tomorrow you will be killed." 12 So Michal let David down through a window. And he went and fled and escaped. 13 And Michal took an image and laid it in the bed, put a cover of goats' hair for his head, and covered it with clothes. 14 So when Saul sent messengers to take David, she said, "He is sick."

15 Then Saul sent the messengers back to see David, saying, "Bring him up to me in the bed, that I may kill him." 16 And when the messengers had come in, there was the image in the bed, with a cover of goats' hair for his head. 17 Then Saul said to Michal, "Why have you deceived me like this, and sent my enemy away, so that he has escaped?"

And Michal answered Saul, "He said to me, 'Let me go! Why should I kill you?'"

18 So David fled and escaped, and went to Samuel at Ramah, and told him all that Saul had done to him. And he and Samuel went and stayed in Naioth. 19 Now it was told Saul, saying, "Take note, David is at Naioth in Ramah!" 20 Then Saul sent messengers to take David. And when they saw the group of prophets prophesying, and Samuel standing as leader over them, the Spirit of God came upon the messengers of Saul, and they also prophesied. 21 And when Saul was told, he sent other messengers, and they prophesied likewise. Then Saul sent messengers again the third time, and they prophesied also. 22 Then he also went to Ramah, and came to the great well that is at Sechu. So he asked, and said, "Where are Samuel and David?"

And someone said, "Indeed they are at Naioth in Ramah." 23 So he went there to Naioth in Ramah. Then the Spirit of God was upon him also, and he went on and prophesied until he came to Naioth in Ramah. 24 And he also stripped off his clothes and prophesied before Samuel in like manner, and lay down naked all that day and all that night. Therefore they say, "Is Saul also among the prophets?"

1 Samuel 20:1-42 NKJV

Then David fled from Naioth in Ramah, and went and said to Jonathan, "What have I done? What is my iniquity, and what is my sin before your father, that he seeks my life?"

2 So Jonathan said to him, "By no means! You shall not die! Indeed, my father will do nothing either great or small without first telling me. And why should my father hide this thing from me? It is not so!"

3 Then David took an oath again, and said, "Your father certainly knows that I have found favor in your eyes, and he has said, 'Do not let Jonathan know this, lest he be grieved.' But truly, as the Lord lives and as your soul lives, there is but a step between me and death."

4 So Jonathan said to David, "Whatever you yourself desire, I will do it for you."

5 And David said to Jonathan, "Indeed tomorrow is the New Moon, and I should not fail to sit with the king to eat. But let me go, that I may hide in the field until the third day at evening. 6 If your father misses me at all, then say, 'David earnestly asked permission of me that he might run over to Bethlehem, his city, for there is a yearly sacrifice there for all the family.' 7 If he says thus: 'It is well,' your servant will be safe. But if he is very angry, be sure that evil is determined by him. 8 Therefore you shall deal kindly with your servant, for you have brought your servant into a covenant of the Lord with you. Nevertheless, if there is iniquity in me, kill me yourself, for why should you bring me to your father?"

9 But Jonathan said, "Far be it from you! For if I knew certainly that evil was determined by my father to come upon you, then would I not tell you?"

10 Then David said to Jonathan, "Who will tell me, or what if your father answers you roughly?" 11 And Jonathan said to David, "Come, let us go out into the field." So both of them went out into the field. 12 Then Jonathan said to David: "The Lord God of Israel is witness! When I have sounded out my father sometime tomorrow, or the third day, and indeed there is good toward David, and I do not send to you and tell you, 13 may the Lord do so and much more to Jonathan. But if it pleases my father to do you evil, then I will report it to you and send you away, that you may go in safety. And the Lord be with you as He has been with my father. 14 And you shall not only show me the kindness of the Lord while I still live, that I may not die; 15 but you shall not cut off your kindness from my house forever, no, not when the Lord has cut off every one of the enemies of David from the face of the earth." 16 So Jonathan made a covenant with the house of David, saying, "Let the Lord require it at the hand of David's enemies."

17 Now Jonathan again caused David to vow, because he loved him; for he loved him as he loved his own soul. 18 Then Jonathan said to David, "Tomorrow is the New Moon; and you will be missed, because your seat will be empty. 19 And when you have stayed three days, go down quickly and come to the place where you hid on the day of the deed; and remain by the stone Ezel. 20 Then I will shoot three arrows to the side, as though I shot at a target; 21 and there I will send a lad, saying, 'Go, find the arrows.' If I expressly say to the lad, 'Look, the arrows are on this side of you; get them and come'—then, as the Lord lives, there is safety for you and no harm. 22 But if I say thus to the young man, 'Look, the arrows are beyond you'—go your way, for the Lord has sent you away. 23 And as for the matter which you and I have spoken of, indeed the Lord be between you and me forever."

24 Then David hid in the field. And when the New Moon had come, the king sat down to eat the feast. 25 Now the king sat on his seat, as at other times, on a seat by the wall. And Jonathan arose, and Abner sat by Saul's side, but David's place was empty. 26 Nevertheless Saul did not say anything that day, for he thought, "Something has happened to him; he is unclean, surely he is unclean." 27 And it happened the next day, the second day of the month, that David's place was empty. And Saul said to Jonathan his son, "Why has the son of Jesse not come to eat, either yesterday or today?"

28 So Jonathan answered Saul, "David earnestly asked permission of me to go to Bethlehem. 29 And he said, 'Please let me go, for our family has a sacrifice in the city, and my brother has commanded me to be there. And now, if I have found favor in your eyes, please let me get away and see my brothers.' Therefore he has not come to the king's table."

30 Then Saul's anger was aroused against Jonathan, and he said to him, "You son of a perverse, rebellious woman! Do I not know that you have chosen the son of Jesse to your own shame and to the shame of your mother's nakedness? 31 For as long as the son of Jesse lives on the earth, you shall not be established, nor your kingdom. Now therefore, send and bring him to me, for he shall surely die."

32 And Jonathan answered Saul his father, and said to him, "Why should he be killed? What has he done?" 33 Then Saul cast a spear at him to kill him, by which Jonathan knew that it was determined by his father to kill David.

34 So Jonathan arose from the table in fierce anger, and ate no food the second day of the month, for he was grieved for David, because his father had treated him shamefully.

35 And so it was, in the morning, that Jonathan went out into the field at the time appointed with David, and a little lad was with him. 36 Then he said to his lad, "Now run, find the arrows which I shoot." As the lad ran, he shot an arrow beyond him. 37 When the lad had come to the place where the arrow was which Jonathan had shot, Jonathan cried out after the lad and said, "Is not the arrow beyond you?" 38 And Jonathan cried out after the lad, "Make haste, hurry, do not delay!" So Jonathan's lad gathered up the arrows and came back to his master. 39 But the lad did not know anything. Only Jonathan and David knew of the matter. 40 Then Jonathan gave his weapons to his lad, and said to him, "Go, carry them to the city."

41 As soon as the lad had gone, David arose from a place toward the south, fell on his face to the ground, and bowed down three times. And they kissed one another; and they wept together, but David more so. 42 Then Jonathan said to David, "Go in peace, since we have both sworn in the name of the Lord, saying, 'May the Lord be between you and me, and between your descendants and my descendants, forever." So he arose and departed, and Jonathan went into the city.

1 Samuel 21:1-15 NKJV

Now David came to Nob, to Ahimelech the priest. And Ahimelech was afraid when he met David, and said to him, "Why are you alone, and no one is with you?"

2 So David said to Ahimelech the priest, "The king has ordered me on some business, and said to me, 'Do not let anyone know anything about the business on which I send you, or what I have commanded you.' And I have directed my young men to such and such a place. 3 Now therefore, what have you on hand? Give me five loaves of bread in my hand, or whatever can be found."

4 And the priest answered David and said, "There is no common bread on hand; but there is holy bread, if the young men have at least kept themselves from women."

5 Then David answered the priest, and said to him, "Truly, women have been kept from us about three days since I came out. And the vessels of the young men are holy, and the bread is in effect common, even though it was consecrated in the vessel this day."

6 So the priest gave him holy bread; for there was no bread there but the showbread which had been taken from before the Lord, in order to put hot bread in its place on the day when it was taken away.

7 Now a certain man of the servants of Saul was there that day, detained before the Lord. And his name was Doeg, an Edomite, the chief of the herdsmen who belonged to Saul.

8 And David said to Ahimelech, "Is there not here on hand a spear or a sword? For I have brought neither my sword nor my weapons with me, because the king's business required haste."

9 So the priest said, "The sword of Goliath the Philistine, whom you killed in the Valley of Elah, there it is, wrapped in a cloth behind the ephod. If you will take that, take it. For there is no other except that one here."

And David said, "There is none like it; give it to me."

(David Flees to Gath)

10 Then David arose and fled that day from before Saul, and went to Achish the king of Gath. 11 And the servants of Achish said to him, "Is this not David the king of the land? Did they not sing of him to one another in dances, saying:

'Saul has slain his thousands, And David his ten thousands'?"

12 Now David took these words to heart, and was very much afraid of Achish the king of Gath. 13 So he changed his behavior before them, pretended madness in their hands, scratched on the doors of the gate, and let his saliva fall down on his beard. 14 Then Achish said to his servants, "Look, you see the man is insane. Why have you brought him to me? 15 Have I need of madmen, that you have brought this fellow to play the madman in my presence? Shall this fellow come into my house?"

1 Samuel 22:1-23 NKJV

David therefore departed from there and escaped to the cave of Adullam. So when his brothers and all his father's house heard it, they went down there to him. 2 And everyone who was in distress, everyone who was in debt, and everyone who was discontented gathered to him. So he became captain over them. And there were about four hundred men with him.

3 Then David went from there to Mizpah of Moab; and he said to the king of Moab, "Please let my father and mother come here with you, till I know what God will do for me." 4 So he brought them before the king of Moab, and they dwelt with him all the time that David was in the stronghold.

5 Now the prophet Gad said to David, "Do not stay in the stronghold; depart, and go to the land of Judah." So David departed and went into the forest of Hereth.

Saul Murders the Priests –

6 When Saul heard that David and the men who were with him had been discovered—now Saul was staying in Gibeah under a tamarisk tree in Ramah, with his spear in his hand, and all his servants standing about him— 7 then Saul said to his servants who stood about him, "Hear now, you Benjamites! Will the son of Jesse give every one of you fields and vineyards, and make you all captains of thousands and captains of hundreds? 8 All of you have conspired against me, and there is no one who reveals to me that my son has made a covenant with the son of Jesse; and there is not one of you who is sorry for me or reveals to me that my son has stirred up my servant against me, to lie in wait, as it is this day."

9 Then answered Doeg the Edomite, who was set over the servants of Saul, and said, "I saw the son of Jesse going to Nob, to Ahimelech the son of Ahitub. 10 And he inquired of the Lord for him, gave him provisions, and gave him the sword of Goliath the Philistine."

11 So the king sent to call Ahimelech the priest, the son of Ahitub, and all his father's house, the priests who were in Nob. And they all came to the king. 12 And Saul said, "Hear now, son of Ahitub!"

He answered, "Here I am, my lord."

13 Then Saul said to him, "Why have you conspired against me, you and the son of Jesse, in that you have given him bread and a sword, and have inquired of God for him, that he should rise against me, to lie in wait, as it is this day?"

14 So Ahimelech answered the king and said, "And who among all your servants is as faithful as David, who is the king's son-in-law, who goes at your bidding, and is honorable in your house? 15 Did I then begin to inquire of God for him? Far be it from me! Let not the king impute anything to his servant, or to any in the house of my father. For your servant knew nothing of all this, little or much."

16 And the king said, "You shall surely die, Ahimelech, you and all your father's house!" 17 Then the king said to the guards who stood about him, "Turn and kill the priests of the Lord, because their hand also is with David, and because they knew when he fled and did not tell it to me." But the servants of the king would not lift their hands to strike the priests of the Lord. 18 And the king said to Doeg, "You turn and kill the priests!" So Doeg the Edomite turned and struck the priests, and killed on that day eighty-five men who wore a linen ephod. 19 Also Nob, the city of the priests, he struck with the edge of the sword, both men and women, children and nursing infants, oxen and donkeys and sheep—with the edge of the sword.

20 Now one of the sons of Ahimelech the son of Ahitub, named Abiathar, escaped and fled after David. 21 And Abiathar told David that Saul had killed the Lord's priests. 22 So David said to Abiathar, "I knew that day, when Doeg the Edomite was there, that he would surely tell Saul. I have caused the death of all the persons of your father's house. 23 Stay with me; do not fear. For he who seeks my life seeks your life, but with me you shall be safe."

1 Samuel 23:1-29 NKJV

Then they told David, saying, "Look, the Philistines are fighting against Keilah, and they are robbing the threshing floors."

2 Therefore David inquired of the Lord, saying, "Shall I go and attack these Philistines?"

And the Lord said to David, "Go and attack the Philistines, and save Keilah."

3 But David's men said to him, "Look, we are afraid here in Judah. How much more then if we go to Keilah against the armies of the Philistines?" 4 Then David inquired of the Lord once again.

And the Lord answered him and said, "Arise, go down to Keilah. For I will deliver the Philistines into your hand." 5 And David and his men went to Keilah and fought with the Philistines, struck them with a mighty blow, and took away their livestock. So David saved the inhabitants of Keilah.

6 Now it happened, when Abiathar the son of Ahimelech fled to David at Keilah, that he went down with an ephod in his hand.

7 And Saul was told that David had gone to Keilah. So Saul said, "God has delivered him into my hand, for he has shut himself in by entering a town that has gates and bars." 8 Then Saul called all the people together for war, to go down to Keilah to besiege David and his men.

9 When David knew that Saul plotted evil against him, he said to Abiathar the priest, "Bring the ephod here." 10 Then David said, "O Lord God of Israel, Your servant has certainly heard that Saul seeks to come to Keilah to destroy the city for my sake. 11 Will the men of Keilah deliver me into his hand? Will Saul come down, as Your servant has heard? O Lord God of Israel, I pray, tell Your servant."

And the Lord said, "He will come down."

12 Then David said, "Will the men of Keilah deliver me and my men into the hand of Saul?"

And the Lord said, "They will deliver you."

13 So David and his men, about six hundred, arose and departed from Keilah and went wherever they could go. Then it was told Saul that David had escaped from Keilah; so he halted the expedition.

David in Wilderness Strongholds

14 And David stayed in strongholds in the wilderness, and remained in the mountains in the Wilderness of Ziph. Saul sought him every day, but God did not deliver him into his hand. 15 So David saw that Saul had come out to seek his life. And David was in the Wilderness of Ziph in a forest. 16 Then Jonathan, Saul's son, arose and went to David in the woods and] strengthened his hand in God. 17 And he said to him, "Do not fear, for the hand of Saul my father shall not find you. You shall be king over Israel, and I shall be next to you. Even my father Saul knows that." 18 So the two of them made a covenant before the Lord. And David stayed in the woods, and Jonathan went to his own house.

19 Then the Ziphites came up to Saul at Gibeah, saying, "Is David not hiding with us in strongholds in the woods, in the hill of Hachilah, which is on the south of Jeshimon? 20

Now therefore, O king, come down according to all the desire of your soul to come down; and our part shall be to deliver him into the king's hand."

21 And Saul said, "Blessed are you of the Lord, for you have compassion on me. 22 Please go and find out for sure, and see the place where his hideout is, and who has seen him there. For I am told he is very crafty. 23 See therefore, and take knowledge of all the lurking places where he hides; and come back to me with certainty, and I will go with you. And it shall be, if he is in the land, that I will search for him throughout all the clans of Judah."

24 So they arose and went to Ziph before Saul. But David and his men were in the Wilderness of Maon, in the plain on the south of Jeshimon. 25 When Saul and his men went to seek him, they told David. Therefore he went down to the rock, and stayed in the Wilderness of Maon. And when Saul heard that, he pursued David in the Wilderness of Maon. 26 Then Saul went on one side of the mountain, and David and his men on the other side of the mountain. So David made haste to get away from Saul, for Saul and his men were encircling David and his men to take them.

27 But a messenger came to Saul, saying, "Hurry and come, for the Philistines have invaded the land!" 28 Therefore Saul returned from pursuing David, and went against the Philistines; so they called that place the Rock of Escape. 29 Then David went up from there and dwelt in strongholds at En Gedi.

1 Samuel 24:1-22 NKJV

Now it happened, when Saul had returned from following the Philistines, that it was told him, saying, "Take note! David is in the Wilderness of En Gedi." 2 Then Saul took three thousand chosen men from all Israel, and went to seek David and his men on the Rocks of the Wild Goats. 3 So he came to the sheepfolds by the road, where there was a cave; and Saul went in to attend to his needs. (David and his men were staying in the recesses of the cave.) 4 Then the men of David said to him, "This is the day of which the Lord said to you, 'Behold, I will deliver your enemy into your hand, that you may do to him as it seems good to you.'" And David arose and secretly cut off a corner of Saul's robe. 5 Now it happened afterward that David's heart troubled him because he had cut Saul's robe. 6 And he said to his men, "The Lord forbid that I should do this thing to my master, the Lord's anointed, to stretch out my hand against him, seeing he is the anointed of the Lord." 7 So David restrained his servants with these words, and did not allow them to rise against Saul. And Saul got up from the cave and went on his way.

8 David also arose afterward, went out of the cave, and called out to Saul, saying, "My lord the king!" And when Saul looked behind him, David stooped with his face to the earth, and bowed down. 9 And David said to Saul: "Why do you listen to the words of men who say, 'Indeed David seeks your harm'? 10 Look, this day your eyes have seen that the Lord

delivered you today into my hand in the cave, and someone urged me to kill you. But my eye spared you, and I said, 'I will not stretch out my hand against my lord, for he is the Lord's anointed.' 11 Moreover, my father, see! Yes, see the corner of your robe in my hand! For in that I cut off the corner of your robe, and did not kill you, know and see that there is neither evil nor rebellion in my hand, and I have not sinned against you. Yet you hunt my life to take it. 12 Let the Lord judge between you and me, and let the Lord avenge me on you. But my hand shall not be against you. 13 As the proverb of the ancients says, 'Wickedness proceeds from the wicked.' But my hand shall not be against you. 14 After whom has the king of Israel come out?

Whom do you pursue? A dead dog? A flea? 15 Therefore let the Lord be judge, and judge between you and me, and see and plead my case, and deliver me out of your hand."

16 So it was, when David had finished speaking these words to Saul, that Saul said, "Is this your voice, my son David?" And Saul lifted up his voice and wept. 17 Then he said to David: "You are more righteous than I; for you have rewarded me with good, whereas I have rewarded you with evil. 18 And you have shown this day how you have dealt well with me; for when the Lord delivered me into your hand, you did not kill me. 19 For if a man finds his enemy, will he let him get away safely? Therefore may the Lord reward you with good for what you have done to me this day. 20 And now I know indeed that you shall surely be king, and that the kingdom of Israel shall be established in your hand. 21 Therefore swear now to me by the Lord that you will not cut off my descendants after me, and that you will not destroy my name from my father's house."

22 So David swore to Saul. And Saul went home, but David and his men went up to the stronghold.

1 Samuel 25:1-44 NKJV

Death of Samuel

1 Then Samuel died; and the Israelites gathered together and lamented for him, and buried him at his home in Ramah. And David arose and went down to the Wilderness of Paran.

David and the Wife of Nabal

2 Now there was a man in Maon whose business was in Carmel, and the man was very rich. He had three thousand sheep and a thousand goats. And he was shearing his sheep in Carmel. 3 The name of the man was Nabal, and the name of his wife Abigail. And she was a woman of good understanding and beautiful appearance; but the man was harsh and evil in his doings. He was of the house of Caleb.

4 When David heard in the wilderness that Nabal was shearing his sheep, 5 David sent ten young men; and David said to the young men, "Go up to Carmel, go to Nabal, and greet him in my name. 6 And thus you shall say to him who lives in prosperity: 'Peace be to you, peace to your house, and peace to all that you have! 7 Now I have heard that you have shearers. Your shepherds were with us, and we did not hurt them, nor was there anything missing from them all the while they were in Carmel. 8 Ask your young men, and they will tell you. Therefore let my young men find favor in your eyes, for we come on a feast day. Please give whatever comes to your hand to your servants and to your son David.'"

9 So when David's young men came, they spoke to Nabal according to all these words in the name of David, and waited.

10 Then Nabal answered David's servants, and said, "Who is David, and who is the son of Jesse? There are many servants nowadays who break away each one from his master. 11 Shall I then take my bread and my water and my meat that I have killed for my shearers, and give it to men when I do not know where they are from?"

12 So David's young men turned on their heels and went back; and they came and told him all these words. 13 Then David said to his men, "Every man gird on his sword." So every man girded on his sword, and David also girded on his sword. And about four hundred men went with David, and two hundred stayed with the supplies.

14 Now one of the young men told Abigail, Nabal's wife, saying, "Look, David sent messengers from the wilderness to greet our master; and he reviled them. 15 But the men were very good to us, and we were not hurt, nor did we miss anything as long as we accompanied them, when we were in the fields. 16 They were a wall to us both by night and day, all the time we were with them keeping the sheep. 17 Now therefore, know and consider what you will do, for harm is determined against our master and against all his household. For he is such a scoundrel that one cannot speak to him."

18 Then Abigail made haste and took two hundred loaves of bread, two skins of wine, five sheep already dressed, five seahs of roasted grain, one hundred clusters of raisins, and two hundred cakes of figs, and loaded them on donkeys. 19 And she said to her servants, "Go on before me; see, I am coming after you." But she did not tell her husband Nabal.

20 So it was, as she rode on the donkey, that she went down under cover of the hill; and there were David and his men, coming down toward her, and she met them. 21 Now David had said, "Surely in vain I have protected all that this fellow has in the wilderness, so that nothing was missed of all that belongs to him. And he has repaid me evil for good. 22 May God do so, and more also, to the enemies of David, if I leave one male of all who belong to him by morning light."

23 Now when Abigail saw David, she dismounted quickly from the donkey, fell on her face before David, and bowed down to the ground. 24 So she fell at his feet and said: "On me, my lord, on me let this iniquity be! And please let your maidservant speak in your ears, and hear the words of your maidservant. 25 Please, let not my lord regard this scoundrel Nabal. For as his name is, so is he: Nabal is his name, and folly is with him! But I, your maidservant, did not see the young men of my lord whom you sent. 26 Now therefore, my lord, as the Lord lives and as your soul lives, since the Lord has held you back from coming to bloodshed and from avenging yourself with your own hand, now then, let your enemies and those who seek harm for my lord be as Nabal. 27 And now this present which your maidservant has brought to my lord, let it be given to the young men who follow my lord. 28 Please forgive the trespass of your maidservant. For the Lord will certainly make for my lord an enduring house, because my lord fights the battles of the Lord, and evil is not found in you throughout your days. 29 Yet a man has risen to pursue you and seek your life, but the life of my lord shall be bound in the bundle of the living with the Lord your God; and the lives of your enemies He shall sling out, as from the pocket of a sling. 30 And it shall come to pass, when the Lord has done for my lord according to all the good that He has spoken concerning you, and has appointed you ruler over Israel, 31 that this will be no grief to you, nor offense of heart to my lord, either that you have shed blood without cause, or that my lord has avenged himself. But when the Lord has dealt well with my lord, then remember your maidservant."

32 Then David said to Abigail: "Blessed is the Lord God of Israel, who sent you this day to meet me! 33 And blessed is your advice and blessed are you, because you have kept me this day from coming to bloodshed and from avenging myself with my own hand. 34 For indeed, as the Lord God of Israel lives, who has kept me back from hurting you, unless you had hurried and come to meet me, surely by morning light no males would have been left to Nabal!" 35 So David received from her hand what she had brought him, and said to her, "Go up in peace to your house. See, I have heeded your voice and respected your person."

36 Now Abigail went to Nabal, and there he was, holding a feast in his house, like the feast of a king. And Nabal's heart was merry within him, for he was very drunk; therefore she told him nothing, little or much, until morning light. 37 So it was, in the morning, when the wine had gone from Nabal, and his wife had told him these things, that his heart died within him, and he became like a stone. 38 Then it happened, after about ten days, that the Lord struck Nabal, and he died.

39 So when David heard that Nabal was dead, he said, "Blessed be the Lord, who has pleaded the cause of my reproach from the hand of Nabal, and has kept His servant from evil! For the Lord has returned the wickedness of Nabal on his own head."

And David sent and proposed to Abigail, to take her as his wife. 40 When the servants of David had come to Abigail at Carmel, they spoke to her saying, "David sent us to you, to ask you to become his wife."

41 Then she arose, bowed her face to the earth, and said, "Here is your maidservant, a servant to wash the feet of the servants of my lord." 42 So Abigail rose in haste and rode on a donkey, attended by five of her maidens; and she followed the messengers of David, and became his wife. 43 David also took Ahinoam of Jezreel, and so both of them were his wives.

44 But Saul had given Michal his daughter, David's wife, to Palti the son of Laish, who was from Gallim.

1 Samuel 26:1-25 NJKV

David Spares Saul a Second Time

1 Now the Ziphites came to Saul at Gibeah, saying, "Is David not hiding in the hill of Hachilah, opposite Jeshimon?" 2 Then Saul arose and went down to the Wilderness of Ziph, having three thousand chosen men of Israel with him, to seek David in the Wilderness of Ziph. 3 And Saul encamped in the hill of Hachilah, which is opposite Jeshimon, by the road. But David stayed in the wilderness, and he saw that Saul came after him into the wilderness. 4 David therefore sent out spies, and understood that Saul had indeed come.

5 So David arose and came to the place where Saul had encamped. And David saw the place where Saul lay, and Abner the son of Ner, the commander of his army. Now Saul lay within the camp, with the people encamped all around him. 6 Then David answered, and said to Ahimelech the Hittite and to Abishai the son of Zeruiah, brother of Joab, saying, "Who will go down with me to Saul in the camp?"

And Abishai said, "I will go down with you."

7 So David and Abishai came to the people by night; and there Saul lay sleeping within the camp, with his spear stuck in the ground by his head. And Abner and the people lay all around him. 8 Then Abishai said to David, "God has delivered your enemy into your hand this day. Now therefore, please, let me strike him at once with the spear, right to the earth; and I will not have to strike him a second time!"

9 But David said to Abishai, "Do not destroy him; for who can stretch out his hand against the Lord's anointed, and be guiltless?" 10 David said furthermore, "As the Lord lives, the Lord shall strike him, or his day shall come to die, or he shall go out to battle and perish. 11 The Lord forbid that I should stretch out my hand against the Lord's anointed. But

please, take now the spear and the jug of water that are by his head, and let us go." 12 So David took the spear and the jug of water by Saul's head, and they got away; and no man saw or knew it or awoke. For they were all asleep, because a deep sleep from the Lord had fallen on them.

13 Now David went over to the other side, and stood on the top of a hill afar off, a great distance being between them. 14 And David called out to the people and to Abner the son of Ner, saying, "Do you not answer, Abner?"

Then Abner answered and said, "Who are you, calling out to the king?"

15 So David said to Abner, "Are you not a man? And who is like you in Israel? Why then have you not guarded your lord the king? For one of the people came in to destroy your lord the king. 16 This thing that you have done is not good. As the Lord lives, you deserve to die, because you have not guarded your master, the Lord's anointed. And now see where the king's spear is, and the jug of water that was by his head."

17 Then Saul knew David's voice, and said, "Is that your voice, my son David?"

David said, "It is my voice, my lord, O king." 18 And he said, "Why does my lord thus pursue his servant? For what have I done, or what evil is in my hand? 19 Now therefore, please, let my lord the king hear the words of his servant: If the Lord has stirred you up against me, let Him accept an offering. But if it is the children of men, may they be cursed before the Lord, for they have driven me out this day from sharing in the inheritance of the Lord, saying, 'Go, serve other gods.' 20 So now, do not let my blood fall to the earth before the face of the Lord. For the king of Israel has come out to seek a flea, as when one hunts a partridge in the mountains."

21 Then Saul said, "I have sinned. Return, my son David. For I will harm you no more, because my life was precious in your eyes this day. Indeed I have played the fool and erred exceedingly."

22 And David answered and said, "Here is the king's spear. Let one of the young men come over and get it. 23 May the Lord repay every man for his righteousness and his faithfulness; for the Lord delivered you into my hand today, but I would not stretch out my hand against the Lord's anointed. 24 And indeed, as your life was valued much this day in my eyes, so let my life be valued much in the eyes of the Lord, and let Him deliver me out of all tribulation."

25 Then Saul said to David, "May you be blessed, my son David! You shall both do great things and also still prevail."

So David went on his way, and Saul returned to his place.

1 Samuel 30:22-31 NKJV

Then all the wicked and worthless men of those who went with David answered and said, "Because they did not go with us, we will not give them any of the spoil that we have recovered, except for every man's wife and children, that they may lead them away and depart."

23 But David said, "My brethren, you shall not do so with what the Lord has given us, who has preserved us and delivered into our hand the troop that came against us. 24 For who will heed you in this matter? But as his part is who goes down to the battle, so shall his part be who stays by the supplies; they shall share alike." 25 So it was, from that day forward; he made it a statute and an ordinance for Israel to this day.

26 Now when David came to Ziklag, he sent some of the spoil to the elders of Judah, to his friends, saying, "Here is a present for you from the spoil of the enemies of the Lord"— 27 to those who were in Bethel, those who were in Ramoth of the South, those who were in Jattir, 28 those who were in Aroer, those who were in Siphmoth, those who were in Eshtemoa, 29 those who were in Rachal, those who were in the cities of the Jerahmeelites, those who were in the cities of the Kenites, 30 those who were in Hormah, those who were in Chorashan, those who were in Athach, 31 those who were in Hebron, and to all the places where David himself and his men were accustomed to rove.

2 Samuel 9:1-13 NKJV

David's Kindness to Mephibosheth

1 Now David said, "Is there still anyone who is left of the house of Saul, that I may show him [a]kindness for Jonathan's sake?"

2 And *there was* a servant of the house of Saul whose name *was* Ziba. So when they had called him to David, the king said to him, "*Are* you Ziba?"

He said, "At your service!"

3 Then the king said, "*Is* there not still someone of the house of Saul, to whom I may show the kindness of God?"

And Ziba said to the king, "There is still a son of Jonathan *who is* lame in *his* feet."

4 So the king said to him, "Where *is* he?"

And Ziba said to the king, "Indeed he is in the house of Machir the son of Ammiel, in Lo Debar."

140

5 Then King David sent and brought him out of the house of Machir the son of Ammiel, from Lo Debar.

6 Now when Mephibosheth the son of Jonathan, the son of Saul, had come to David, he fell on his face and prostrated himself. Then David said, "Mephibosheth?"

And he answered, "Here is your servant!"

7 So David said to him, "Do not fear, for I will surely show you kindness for Jonathan your father's sake, and will restore to you all the land of Saul your grandfather; and you shall eat bread at my table continually."

8 Then he bowed himself, and said, "What is your servant, that you should look upon such a dead dog as I?"

9 And the king called to Ziba, Saul's servant, and said to him, "I have given to your master's son all that belonged to Saul and to all his house.

10 You therefore, and your sons and your servants, shall work the land for him, and you shall bring in the harvest, that your master's son may have food to eat. But Mephibosheth your master's son shall eat bread at my table always." Now Ziba had fifteen sons and twenty servants.

11 Then Ziba said to the king, "According to all that my lord the king has commanded his servant, so will your servant do."

"As for Mephibosheth," said the king, "he shall eat at my table like one of the king's sons." 12 Mephibosheth had a young son whose name was Micha. And all who dwelt in the house of Ziba were servants of Mephibosheth. 13 So Mephibosheth dwelt in Jerusalem, for he ate continually at the king's table. And he was lame in both his feet.

2 Samuel 12:1-10 NKJV

Nathan's Parable and David's Confession

1 Then the Lord sent Nathan to David. And he came to him, and said to him: "There were two men in one city, one rich and the other poor. 2 The rich man had exceedingly many flocks and herds. 3 But the poor man had nothing, except one little ewe lamb which he had bought and nourished; and it grew up together with him and with his children. It ate of his own food and drank from his own cup and lay in his bosom; and it was like a daughter to him. 4 And a traveler came to the rich man, who refused to take from his own flock and from his own herd to prepare one for the wayfaring man who had come to him; but he took the poor man's lamb and prepared it for the man who had come to him."

5 So David's anger was greatly aroused against the man, and he said to Nathan, "As the Lord lives, the man who has done this shall surely die! 6 And he shall restore fourfold for the lamb, because he did this thing and because he had no pity."

7 Then Nathan said to David, "You are the man! Thus says the Lord God of Israel: 'I anointed you king over Israel, and I delivered you from the hand of Saul. 8 I gave you your master's house and your master's wives into your keeping, and gave you the house of Israel and Judah. And if that had been too little, I also would have given you much more! 9 Why have you despised the commandment of the Lord, to do evil in His sight? You have killed Uriah the Hittite with the sword; you have taken his wife to be your wife, and have killed him with the sword of the people of Ammon. 10 Now therefore, the sword shall never depart from your house, because you have despised Me, and have taken the wife of Uriah the Hittite to be your wife.'

2 Samuel 16:1-4 NKJV

Mephibosheth's Servant

1 When David was a little past the top *of the mountain,* there was Ziba the servant of Mephibosheth, who met him with a couple of saddled donkeys, and on them two hundred *loaves* of bread, one hundred clusters of raisins, one hundred summer fruits, and a skin of wine. 2 And the king said to Ziba, "What do you mean to do with these?"

2 So Ziba said, "The donkeys *are* for the king's household to ride on, the bread and summer fruit for the young men to eat, and the wine for those who are faint in the wilderness to drink."

3 Then the king said, "And where *is* your master's son?"

And Ziba said to the king, "Indeed he is staying in Jerusalem, for he said, 'Today the house of Israel will restore the kingdom of my father to me."

4 So the king said to Ziba, "Here, all that *belongs* to Mephibosheth *is* yours."

And Ziba said, "I humbly bow before you, *that* I may find favor in your sight, my lord, O king!"

ATTACHMENTS

Proposed Schedule

Workshops can be planned in sessions for 1 ½ to 2 hours; example, 12:00pm – 2:00pm
Sessions include book and presentations by a facilitator.

MONTH	ACTIVITIES	PERSON(S)	COMPLETE / FOLLOW-UP
January	Schedule Meeting with Pastor & Facilitator Introduce Program to Church Body & Leaders	Administration Coordinator Pastor	
February	Conduct Pre-Assessments Establish Dates for assessing and completion	Administration Coordinator	
	Establish/review protocol for summarizing assessments with Pastor and Tallying Team	Administration Coordinator	
SECTION II: CHARACTER/TRAITS			
March - April	Teams read, research and complete activities 1-8 related to the topic of character traits.	Workshop Facilitator	
SECTION III: CHARACTER OF A LEADER			
May - July	Teams read, research and complete activities 1-8 related to the topic of character of leaders called by God.	Workshop Facilitator	
SECTION IV: RESPONSBILE SERVANT LEADERSHIP			
July - August	Teams read, research and complete activities 1-6 related to the topic of character of responsible servant leadership that pleases God.	Workshop Facilitator	

SECTION V: UNLIKELY SERVANT LEADERS			
August	Teams read, research and complete activities 1-4 related to unlikely servant leaders	Workshop Facilitator	
September & October	Experiential Learning Post Assessments	Church Body and Leaders Administrator Coordinator	
October	Leadership Day & Ceremonial Graduation Celebration	Administrator Coordinator with Team	
November& December	Post Assessments: Review and address areas of concerns; target goals to ensure the focus is always on God's agenda as individuals and the Church Body.	Pastor with Leadership Team	

Summarizing Individual Pastoral Ministry Assessments

PERSONAL LIFE of the pastor						
The pastor gives evidence of:						
1. A deep commitment to Christ and a godly lifestyle.	1	2	3	4	5	6
2. A competent knowledge of the Bible	1	2	3	4	5	6
3. A love for the work of the church.	1	2	3	4	5	6
4. A concern and compassion for unbelievers	1	2	3	4	5	6
5. An active prayer life	1	2	3	4	5	6
HOME LIFE (where applicable)						
6. Takes time with spouse and family.	1	2	3	4	5	6
7. Spouse and family support the ministry.	1	2	3	4	5	6

HOME LIFE (where applicable) Continued						
8. Models a loving home life.	1	2	3	4	5	6
9. Good balance between work & leisure	1	2	3	4	5	6
10. Allows for recreational time.	1	2	3	4	5	6
AS A LEADER the pastor						
11. Is effective in communicating the vision and goals of the church.	1	2	3	4	5	6
12. Models good time management	1	2	3	4	5	6
13. Models a spirit of love and a servant attitude.	1	2	3	4	5	6
14. Accepts suggestions well.	1	2	3	4	5	6

AS A LEADER *(Continued) the pastor*						
15. Supports conference & denominational ministries.	1	2	3	4	5	6
16. Is effective in equipping and empowering the people for ministry.	1	2	3	4	5	6
17. Is aware of and sensitive to peoples' needs.	1	2	3	4	5	6
AS A COMMUNICATOR *the pastor*						
18. Encourages and challenges me to grow spiritually and mature in my faith.	1	2	3	4	5	6
19. Models the value of prayer.	1	2	3	4	5	6
20. Supports participation in the service.	1	2	3	4	5	6
AS A COMMUNICATOR *(Continued) the pastor*						
21. Is biblical and relevant in preaching.	1	2	3	4	5	6
22. Helps me apply biblical truth to my daily life.	1	2	3	4	5	6
23. Is compelling and persuasive in his/her style of delivery.	1	2	3	4	5	6
AS AN ADVISOR/COUNSELLOR *the pastor*						
24. Is easy to talk to.	1	2	3	4	5	6
25. Is a good listener.	1	2	3	4	5	6
26. Is perceptive and understands me.	1	2	3	4	5	6
27. Provides wise counsel and direction.	1	2	3	4	5	6
28. Admits to limits readily.	1	2	3	4	5	6

Question#	What is the highest count for each question?						
Plotting Your Data – Alternate Form Name of Assessment _____ Date _____							
1.	1	2	3	4	5	6	High Score
2.	1	2	3	4	5	6	
3.	1	2	3	4	5	6	
4.	1	2	3	4	5	6	
5.	1	2	3	4	5	6	
6.	1	2	3	4	5	6	
7.	1	2	3	4	5	6	
8.	1	2	3	4	5	6	
9.	1	2	3	4	5	6	
10.	1	2	3	4	5	6	
11.	1	2	3	4	5	6	

	Plotting Your Data – Alternate Form						
	Name of Assessment _____ . Date _____						
Question#	What is the highest count for each question?						
12.	1	2	3	4	5	6	
13.	1	2	3	4	5	6	
14.	1	2	3	4	5	6	
15.	1	2	3	4	5	6	
16.	1	2	3	4	5	6	
17.	1	2	3	4	5	6	
18.	1	2	3	4	5	6	
19.	1	2	3	4	5	6	
20.	1	2	3	4	5	6	
21.	1	2	3	4	5	6	
22.	1	2	3	4	5	6	

	Plotting Your Data – Alternate Form						
	Name of Assessment _____ Date _____						
Question#	What is the highest count for each question?						
23.	1	2	3	4	5	6	
24.	1	2	3	4	5	6	
25.	1	2	3	4	5	6	
26.	1	2	3	4	5	6	
27.	1	2	3	4	5	6	
28.	1	2	3	4	5	6	
29.	1	2	3	4	5	6	
30.	1	2	3	4	5	6	

Summarizing Assessment Results

Name of Assessment_____

Number of Questions: _____   **Date:** _____

STRENGTHS – HIGHEST THREE SCORES

QUESTION# _____

QUESTION# _____

QUESTION# _____

CHALLENGES – LOWEST THREE SCORES

QUESTION# _____

QUESTION# _____

QUESTION# _____

Summarizing Form For Individual Church Ministry

30 QUESTIONS

WORSHIP

1. The worship services help us focus our attention on God and His Word.	1	2	3	4	5	6
2. The worship services are uplifting.	1	2	3	4	5	6
3. The style of worship meets the needs and goals of our church.	1	2	3	4	5	6
4. Prayer is viewed as an important part of worship in the church.	1	2	3	4	5	6

PREACHING/TEACHING

5. Is biblical and relevant to daily life.	1	2	3	4	5	6
6. Provides a clear understanding of God's word.	1	2	3	4	5	6
7. Encourages spiritual growth.	1	2	3	4	5	6
8. Is challenging and motivating.	1	2	3	4	5	6

VISION/LEADERSHIP						
9. The church's vision/mission statement is clearly communicated and known.	1	2	3	4	5	6
10. The pastor & staff have a good working relationship with the church leadership.	1	2	3	4	5	6
11. The leaders are sensitive to the needs of the members and seek their input.	1	2	3	4	5	6
12. Leaders are chosen basis on their spiritual qualifications and ability to lead.	1	2	3	4	5	6
13. I support and regularly pray for our church leaders.	1	2	3	4	5	6
ADMINISTRATION/ORGANIZATION						
14. The organizational structure is effective with clear lines of responsibility/ accountability.	1	2	3	4	5	6
15. Events and services are organized well.	1	2	3	4	5	6
16. Members' needs are cared for through the ministry of the church.	1	2	3	4	5	6

DISCIPLESHIP/EQUIPPING						
17. Spiritual growth is taking place through small groups, classes, etc.	1	2	3	4	5	6
18. The church is effective in helping new Christians grow in their faith.	1	2	3	4	5	6
19. Growing in Christlikeness is highly valued and fostered in the church.	1	2	3	4	5	6
20. Training is provided for the various ministries of the church.	1	2	3	4	5	6
21. People are challenged to be involved in ministry and their gifts are affirmed.	1	2	3	4	5	6
22. The purpose of each ministry program is clearly stated.	1	2	3	4	5	6
23. There is a sense of purpose and direction in reaching our community.	1	2	3	4	5	6
24. Members show a desire to share Christ with their friends.	1	2	3	4	5	6

EVANGELISM/MISSIONS						
25. People are coming to Christ through the ministry of the church.	1	2	3	4	5	6
26. The church is committed in prayer and financially to world missions.	1	2	3	4	5	6
27. A good percentage of the church budget is designated for missions.	1	2	3	4	5	6
STEWARDSHIP/FINANCES						
28. The budget appropriately reflects the church's vision and goals for ministry.	1	2	3	4	5	6
29. Biblical stewardship is frequently and effectively taught.	1	2	3	4	5	6
30. Members are committed to give proportionally of their income to the church budget.	1	2	3	4	5	6

What are some, if any, known apprehensions?

_____

_____

_____

_____

In what area(s) do you think there is a need for the Church to consider?

_____

_____

_____

What should be the response of the servant leader?

_____

_____

_____

Individual Ministry Post Self-Assessment

Page 1 of 2

This assessment will help you reflect on your support of the ministry. Consider your personal strengths and weaknesses. I pray you will recognize the value of your importance to maintaining a healthy, effective ministry.

Numeric Scale:

1 = Disagree Strongly	**2 = Disagree**	**3 = Disagree Somewhat**
4 = Agree Somewhat	**5 = Agree**	**6 = Agree Strongly**

NOTE: Leave blank if not applicable.

WORSHIP						
1. I attend worship services to focus on God and His Word.	1	2	3	4	5	6
2. I pray daily for our congregation.	1	2	3	4	5	6
3. I pray for the worship services.	1	2	3	4	5	6
4. I celebrate and praise God without hesitation.	1	2	3	4	5	6
5. I pray that the Holy Spirit guide me in worship.	1	2	3	4	5	6
PREACHING/TEACHING						
6. I pray for God's people to have an attentive ear for God's Word.	1	2	3	4	5	6
7. I attend church education classes.	1	2	3	4	5	6
8. I attend church classes to help understand God's Word.	1	2	3	4	5	6
9. I pray for preaching/teaching that edifies the church.	1	2	3	4	5	6
10. I study God's Word in private to hear from God.	1	2	3	4	5	6
VISION/LEADERSHIP						
11. I know the vision/mission of the church.	1	2	3	4	5	6
12. I have a good working relationship with the church leadership.	1	2	3	4	5	6
13. I am sensitive to how I speak to members.	1	2	3	4	5	6
14. I speak positively about church leadership outside of the church.	1	2	3	4	5	6
15. I support and regularly pray for our church leaders.	1	2	3	4	5	6
ADMINISTRATION/ORGANIZATION						
16. I spiritually contribute to the growth of the church.	1	2	3	4	5	6
17. I financially support the growth of the ministry.	1	2	3	4	5	6
18. I address concerns about the church through established channels.	1	2	3	4	5	6

Individual Ministry Post Self - Assessment

Page 2 of 2

DISCIPLESHIP/EQUIPPING						
19. I look for ways to support ministry through small groups, classes, etc.	1	2	3	4	5	6
20. I am equipped to help new Christians grow in their faith.	1	2	3	4	5	6
21. I pray and look for ways to develop my skills and gifts.	1	2	3	4	5	6
22. I encourage others to support the ministry.	1	2	3	4	5	6
23. I pray for the right way to handle situations that are harmful to the Body.	1	2	3	4	5	6
24. I share in decisions that lead to constructive ways.	1	2	3	4	5	6
EVANGELISM/MISSIONS						
25. I pray for the creation and equipping of ministry for spiritual, emotional and financial growth in support of a strong healthy community.	1	2	3	4	5	6
26. I share Christ with people to help them grow in faith.	1	2	3	4	5	6
27. I pray and support systems invited by the Holy Spirit that will bring people to Christ.	1	2	3	4	5	6
STEWARDSHIP/FINANCES						
28. I pray for the understanding of stewardship according to the Word of God.	1	2	3	4	5	6
29. I pray for a budget that will positive reflect the goals for ministry.	1	2	3	4	5	6
30. I pray for stewardship that is frequent and effectively taught in the church.	1	2	3	4	5	6

Additional Comments:

Signature _____ *Date*_____

Conclusion

This work was produced to support ministry leaders as Servant Leaders. A servant leader plays a purposeful role in the Kingdom of God. One must be on God's agenda – not a personal agenda. However, God's agenda will generate a personal reward that is everlasting. A servant leader must be equipped by the Holy Spirit. God has given His people the power of the Holy Spirit as our guide. Under the influence of the Holy Spirit, a servant leader will produce summer fruit; it will harvest a great crop for the kingdom; it will be assessed not in number but in quality. The servant leader will labor with fellow workers, tearing up fallow ground, tilling the soil, and sowing seeds that will produce a great harvest in due season. The due season is NOW! Now is the time to "Do Good!" Such is the call of Servant leader NOW.

By the calling of the Holy Spirit, I invite you to engage and equip others for the Kingdom. Encourage, evangelize and inspire for the glory of God – His agenda is to promoted and celebrated NOW - Stepping up to your leadership call!

Bibliography

Ashford, S. J., Heslin, P., & Keating, L. (2017, August 10). Good leaders are good learners. Harvard Business Review. Retrieved from https://hbr.org/2017/08/good-leaders-are-good-learners

Blackaby, H. & Blackaby, R. (2001). *Spiritual leadership.* Nashville, Tennessee: Broadman & Holman Publishers

Carter, Jimmy. (2006). *Our endangered values: America's moral crisis.* New York: Simon Schuster

Ho, M. (2016, May 12). New research shows investing in experiential learning for leaders pays-off. *Association for Talent Development.* Retrieved from https://www.td.org/insights/new-research-shows-investing-in-experiential-learning-for-leaders-pays-off

Northern Plains Region Baptist Conference. (2012, July). Ministry assessment instrument. *Annual Conference.* Retrieved from http://npregion.org/wp-content/uploads/2012/07/Assessment-Guide.pdf

Obama, B. (2019, January 31). *Quotes.* Retrieved January 31, 2019 from https://www.goodreads.com/author/quotes/6356.Barack_Obama

The Holy Bible New International Version (NIV) Cultural Backgrounds Study Bible. (2016). Grand Rapids: Zondervan

White, A. T. (1999). *Twelve commandments for people who work with people.* Cowpens, SC: Threadgill Press

Winfrey, O. (2014). *What I know for sure.* New York: FlatIron Books. Retrieved March 01, 2019 from https://www.goodreads.com/author/quotes/3518.Oprah_Winfrey

Y Scouts. (2019, April 24). *Ten servant leadership traits.* Retrieved from https://yscouts.com/10-servant-leadership-characteristics/

About the Author

Rev. Gardenia T. Bulluck, ACS, BCh.M., M.S. Ed.S.

Gardenia T. Bulluck enjoys sharing the Word of God to bring people to Christ. Since 2004, she has been active in ministry as a co-laborer in church leadership. She glorifies God for this call and inspiration. She is a wife, mother, grandmother, writer, retired public school educator, Christian Educator, and ordained minister. She has been an entrepreneur in the non-profit sector working with families and children for improving literacy. She received her bachelor's degree in business management from Shaw University in Raleigh, North Carolina. She received her Master and Specialist Degrees in Education from Barry University of Miami, Florida. Rev. Bulluck completed her biblical studies degrees in Christian Studies and Church Ministry from the Sure Foundation Theological Institute of Seminole, Florida. She is currently pursuing her Doctorate Degree in Ministry from Northwestern Theological Seminary of New Port Richey, Florida.

www.ingramcontent.com/pod-product-compliance
Lightning Source LLC
Chambersburg PA
CBHW080507110426
42742CB00017B/3022